CHRIS,

REMEMBER WHO YOU ARE AND WHERE YOU CAME FROM. STAY ON YOUR TOES AND ALWAYS KEEP A SMILE ON YOUR FACE!

Smitty

Looking Back

Sgt. Larry Smith (Ret.)

authorHOUSE®

AuthorHouse™
1663 Liberty Drive
Bloomington, IN 47403
www.authorhouse.com
Phone: 1-800-839-8640

©2010 Sgt. Larry Smith (Ret.). All rights reserved.

No part of this book may be reproduced, stored in a retrieval system, or transmitted by any means without the written permission of the author.

First published by AuthorHouse 5/3/2010

ISBN: 978-1-4520-1427-2 (e)
ISBN: 978-1-4520-1428-9 (sc)

Printed in the United States of America
Bloomington, Indiana

This book is printed on acid-free paper.

Dedication

My sincere thanks and gratitude go out to my mother who always told her children that there were no limits in this world. We are only bound by our own imagination and desire to work towards a goal.

And in the course of our lives, each day our footprints cross the footprints of countless others around us. In most cases, these chance encounters are forgotten within seconds if even noticed at all. But when one of these footprints belong to an impressionable young person, it may result in a life-altering genesis. In the late seventies, a friendly municipal police officer named Lindal Marsh left such impressions on those around him. His friendly smile and caring manner spoke volumes of his professionalism and love for what he had committed his life to. It was no wonder younger men looked up to and wanted to be like him. Officer Marsh, I hope I've measured up. God Bless and thank you!

And what a privilege it was to work beside those who are now *"off duty"*.

May God embrace and keep you!

The Cat	*Clarence*
Sammy	*Woody*
C. Bunch	*Ron*
Jimmy	*Tim*
Boone	*Dave*
Boone Jr.	*& Doc*

Forward

The road you travel in life can only be determined by where you want to eventually wind up. This book may help in some small way. **Some of the officer's names along with the agency's name have been changed to honor and respect their right to privacy and for their safety.** I'd also like to express the following sentiments that I consider paramount.

Within the account of my three decades in law-enforcement and my personal experiences during that time, one may (from time to time) get the impression or come to the conclusion that I may have disliked or had a low opinion of one or two particular people or officers. **Let me make something perfectly clear.** Law-enforcement is a grueling career that taxes not only one's physical being but their very soul every minute of every day. Law enforcement officers are human beings and are subject to all the human frailties' and weaknesses like every other human. Dealing with humanity's worse examples every day tends to drains you like the sucking of sap from a tree. Like everyone else, the officers I mention have families, bills, good days and bad. But unlike other occupations where others get to leave the workplace, these people are always "on the clock" and are recognized by their neighbors and strangers alike as someone who can be approached 24/7 for help. To be gotten out of bed in the wee hours because your neighbor heard a noise and chose to give you a call because they didn't want to bother the authorities with something that small is not uncommon. To simply eat a meal in public without someone wanting free legal advice or to air a beef because they got a traffic ticket is everyday. And to walk into a party or social gathering and try to stay "small" without someone shouting, "I didn't do it" or "Look out it's the man" at the top of their lungs and think it's funny is expected.

A law-enforcement officer's primary job is "take control" when "control" has been lost. Simply put, when shots ring out and others run from the origin of fire, this person instinctively runs toward it with no regard for his/her life with the hopes of saving lives, even at the cost of their own. Like some conditioned laboratory rat, these people have something in their blood that separates them from the general population. They are in essence the sheep dogs that stand watch and keep the flock safe from the ever present and watchful eyes of the wolves of society. And if one ever finds themselves among the ranks of law-enforcement as brethren, they will find themselves in a close-knit family like no other. And like siblings in a family, each will squabble, pick, complain, laugh, cry and support each other when the chips are down. I can honestly say that I have never doubted the bravery or willingness of **any** fellow officer to lay down their life for me in the event the call was made, and there have been many!

Those who do not fit this description are soon weeded out from the ranks. And for this reason, we are permitted by each other to squabble and poke fun at each other. But this is a privilege reserved **only** for those who have stood side by side in the trenches and sewers of society.

This philosophy or code if you will applies to and encompasses law-enforcement from our Federal Law Enforcement Officers down to our one man Town Marshal's in rural America. Transportation Officers, Resource Officers and everyone in between are on the front lines daily. Our uniforms may be of different color and our patches of different design but we all share the same every day fears and desire to make a difference. I am proud of each and every man and woman that I've worked with and will always have the warmest of memories and utmost respect for them and the contributions and sacrifices they made. For those who are still on the job and for those who are looking down on us from a much nicer "beat", God Bless and protect you.

Sgt. Larry Smith (Ret.)

The Seed

I was more or less raised by a single mother who worked very hard to raise her three children. She strived to instill attributes and virtues in each of us like hard work, charity, honesty, family, and faith. As we all grew into adulthood, my siblings one by one settled upon a vocation or career that they thought best for them. My older brother John liked working with his hands. My earliest memory of John goes back to watching him glue together model cars, military vehicles, and pretty much anything he could get his hands on. His room was filled with them. I always thought he was a little crazy, but now that I think about it, it may have been the noxious fumes from the glue that accounted for some of the nutty things he later did. If so, at least "he" had an excuse. So when John became a skilled welder for a large corporation, it was no surprise to anyone. To this day, he still loves getting his hands dirty tearing things apart, smelling the noxious cleaning fluid fumes and putting them back together.

My sister Judy, the youngest and Mom's favorite I might add, was the most out-going child. She and I, due to circumstances beyond our control, bounced around the eastern half of the United States with Mom as kids. We seldom stayed in one place for more than a year or two. Mom was married several times and circumstances dictated numerous moves and changes of schools. It was kind of like being in the 'Witness Protection Program'. Counting college, I can remember attending at least fourteen different public schools. As negative as that may sound, the up side of it was that Sis and I learned how to make friends rather quickly and our social skills were a little more developed than the average kid. Sis was always the caring one and always wanted a little more than a position behind a desk or life in a cubical. It also turns out, as much as I hate to admit it, she was probably the smartest of the three. Sis eventually wound up in the nursing field where she remains today. As far as myself, I've never really sat down with either of my siblings and asked just how they came to choose the vocational paths they did. But if I had, I'm sure there would be a story behind it. And neither has indicated any regret regarding their choice.

I can remember as a youth those who had spent decades in the factories and mills in our hometown and how life for them was much like that of a lab rat. Bells, buzzers and whistles governed your daily routine in these factories. And by the time you reached retirement age, the working conditions from the previous thirty years had left your body ravaged and pretty much useless for anything more than cutting the grass or puttering around the house chipping away at the 'honey to-do list'. And after a few years of retirement fun and games, spending time with the grandchildren etc, it was time for that "dirt nap" and the next generation took over and repeated the cycle. All I knew was I wanted nothing to do with this kind of life and wanted something more but could never place my finger on what it was.

I tried sampling a little bit of everything from the limited job market that was out there. I was the original Al Bundy and sold shoes, I pumped gas, worked for an interior decorator, a florist, construction, a lineman for the C. & O. Railroad, life-guarded, mall security, flipped burgers, worked retail sporting goods and even worked in a fireworks factory for God's sake! Nothing seemed to fill the void and that endless feeling that I had of living the life of a lab rat was quickly becoming a possible reality. While in my mid twenties, I worked for the local municipal park department. There I was assigned to the local reservoir and during the winter months a crew of about six of us would repair and paint park benches, tables, pier decking, trash cans, and anything else broken or wasn't nailed down from the previous year in an old barn like structure that was heated by a wood stove. In the spring, we would assemble and install two or three hundred wooden piers in the icy waters of the lake for the boaters. And in the fall, we would take them out of the water to keep them from freezing and being destroyed by the ice movement. The crew I worked with was quite a bunch. When we actually did work, which was quite often, we worked our ass off. But when things got slow because of the weather or lack of manpower, it was usually a poker game and/or some form of shenanigans that helped pass the time. The foreman, and one of my best friends, was an ex-NBA basketball star named Ron Bonham who had played with the Boston Celtics during their glory days. We spent many days hunting and fishing together and even resided in opposite ends of the same duplex. This made the job pretty easy and enjoyable but it was still a road to nowhere.

In the summer time I life guarded along with six others at the recreational swimming area located on the lake full time. If one could have made a career of that vocation, I would have worked it for free! To be young, athletic, not married, going to Ball State University (the name still kills me) and responsible for keeping an eye on as many as several hundred people at a lake front beach during the hot mid-west summer was the best. What a great job for any young guy. Heck, I was there even on my days off prowling the beach like a raccoon rummaging through a dumpster behind Denny's. I worked there for eight years and would still be there if I hadn't realized that my life was slipping through my fingers and come to my senses. I started as one of the guards, but soon made my way to the prestigious rank of head guard. And from then on, glutinous is about as close as I can come to describing my summers. I was in the Garden of Eden and free to roam about and harvest at my leisure.

It was at this beach that I met Officer Lindal Marsh. He was one of about four municipal police officers that were assigned to the lake. Since the lake came under the city's jurisdiction, the city was responsible for it and the people who utilized it. Officer Marsh would drop in on us from time to time up at the maintenance barn during the winter months or at the beach during the summer. Marsh was always joking and laughing; yet you knew he could mean business if the occasion called for it. He was different compared to most of the other cops I knew. You have to remember that this was the seventies and traditionally *the man* was no friend to us longhair folk.

I knew plenty of other police officers and they had no problem letting you know that they really had no use for any long hair, dope smoking, college punks regardless if you fit that description or not. But if ever there were an 'Officer Friendly,' it was this guy. During the winter months we would huddle around the wood-burning stove in the maintenance barn to keep warm. There, Marsh would share stories of what was going on in town or some humorous incident or a blood and guts experience that would capture our wide-eyed attention. He made us laugh and he tore down that barrier most people had toward police during those years. I can still see his smile.

But sometimes, he would speak of a call he had been on where an innocent child had been killed or needlessly suffered and you could hear his voice crack a little as he spoke. Sometimes he would kind of look downward at the floor to keep others from seeing his eyes tear up until he could regain his composure. He tried to hide the fact that he had a big heart, but it just showed just the same. A lot of law enforcement officers during that period were preoccupied with projecting an image of authority and hardness. I think that came from the lack of training and the old image of the New York and Chicago 'beat' cop. Back then, a new officer would be handed a stick and a gun, pointed in a direction and told to 'go get'em'. The only qualifications for being a cop in the early days of law enforcement were you had to know someone to get hired and it didn't hurt to be big and not too bright. We've come a long way.

The relationship between Officer Marsh and me was shared somewhat with a fellow lifeguard and close friend that also wanted a career in law enforcement, Jack. Jack had a very good leg up on me in that his father and sister were both careered in law enforcement. His father, a municipal officer, had been an officer for years and was closing in on retirement. So Jack had an inside track as well as a good idea of what the job involved and was raised inside the loop. The job should have easily been second natured to him. At some point in time, and I can't really put my finger on it, it was determined by both of us that law enforcement was what we wanted to do with our lives. Jack was a few years younger than me, but we were good friends and shared some great times. As the months passed, Jack eventually obtained a position as a reserve officer on the local police department with the help of Dad. A reserve officer however usually meant security guard or traffic detail duty. But no matter how much pull his father had, or anyone else I knew for that matter, I just could not get my foot in the door in our hometown. For months, Jack and I both subscribed to law enforcement magazines or any other materials that would list any agencies looking for new blood. Jack and I both vowed we would take any position in any location if someone would just give us a chance. In the mean time, I kept plugging away locally. But trying to get hired locally came to an unexpected and abrupt halt when my eyes were opened after things became crystal clear one summer day at City Hall.

The town I came from was about average in size during those years. The population was around eighty to ninety thousand and hosted a good size university along with industry and farming. One summer day, the local newspaper publicized that the municipal police department had six openings that they were looking to fill due to retirements and so forth. The newspaper also advised the city would be testing shortly thereafter to hire and replace those leaving. I was elated but knew that there would be a large turnout for those positions and the competition would be fierce. Several hundred applications were distributed and after sorting out the felons, crack pots and criminally insane, there were 202 applicants who made the cut and would be allowed to test for the six positions. My application was among those.

For the next few weeks, applicants were probed, tested, questioned, researched, put through a physical grilling and placed under the microscope. I thought I had done well and indeed I had. At the end of the testing, I wound up placing fourth (4th) out of the 202 tested! Well, there you go

I thought. I figured six positions and I placed fourth, I've got myself a job! Then the eligibility list was posted. Preferential treatment (nepotism) was and still is out of control in my hometown, even after thirty years. And as a result, the top ten applicants on the list were sons, sons-in-laws, brothers, etc. of local government officials. As I read the list, it was like someone had just pulled the plug and let every bit of hope and enthusiasm out of me and there was nothing that I could do about it. That's just the way it was. Oh by the way, I wound number (54th) on the list after placing (4th) in the testing. I was amazed that there were (53) others who had enough political pull to get in front of me. Damn, now what?

Pinch Me!

It took a couple of months to pull myself up, brush myself off and convince myself to not take no for an answer. Jack was working pretty regular as a Reserve on the local police department, but it really wasn't what he wanted either. Like I said, reserve duty was mostly watchman and special event stuff. Towards the end of the seventies, the country was struggling with the economy as well as with social unrest and racial issues were always present. In some areas of the country, people were just plain lucky to have a job let alone have the job or career they wanted.

For a year or two longer, Jack and I applied at several agencies in and out of the state. I'd work at whatever I could, save money and would travel all over the country taking entry level tests with a hoard of other hopeful applicants for one or two available positions with various departments. Times were tough at best! Finally Jack gave up and moved south to Florida to work with his uncle in Palm Beach, a wealthy inter-coastal island community in Florida. Jack's uncle owned the only gas station on the island and pumping gas in Palm Beach beat the hell out of mid-night shift guard duty at some construction site or hospital parking lot.

I hated to see him go but I was glad he at least got out of Armpit, Indiana. We kept in touch but there wasn't much to talk about locally. The 'good old boy' system made sure of that. Days turned into weeks, weeks into months and Armpit, Indiana was feeling more and more like the La Brea Tar Pits and I was some wild prehistoric animal just trying to get unstuck. It was looking like I would never get out of there and my destiny would be sealed in some cruddy day shift at some factory or maybe, if I was real lucky, owner of a fast food franchise around campus. I wanted to just lie in the middle of the street, *someone please, shoot me!*

Then one day, I got a phone call from Jack who seemed pretty excited. He told me of a city in South Florida called (to keep the attorneys off my tail, we'll call it) Tropical Beach. Tropical Beach was advertising nation wide for applicants for their police department. I should have seen the "red flags" right then and there, but if it made Jack excited, why should I be any different? Jack went on to tell of white sandy beaches, college students and tourists, turquoise water and sunshine year round. Oh yeah, and the starting pay and benefits were pretty good too. I do remember asking if he knew why the city didn't hire from the local population and why were they looking to advertise out of state? He said he really didn't know. He guessed that out of state applicants would probably be more committed once hired and the city thought there would be less of a chance of losing them. That sounded logical to me.

Jack gave me the phone number and contact person's name at the department. Jack said if I came down to Florida, I could stay with him and if we both got ourselves hired, I could live with him until I got started. We were fortunate that the police academy was conveniently just a few minutes from his home in the local community college. That was awful generous of him seeing how Jack had just gotten married. I knew his bride but not very well. I had only met her for a few moments once before he left for Florida. But what the hell, it was the only game in town. With this new breath of hope, it only took a couple of minutes before I was on the phone long distance to the Tropical Beach Police Department inquiring about the positions. I was so excited; I neglected to do any research or make the first inquiry about what kind of place this Tropical Beach was. All I had to know was it wasn't Armpit, Indiana!

When I called the department and asked for information in regards to the hiring of new officers, I was connected with the department's training officer, Sergeant Robins. From the first words spoken by Sergeant Robins, I could tell that this guy was ex-military and was on top of things. The confidence and command poured out of the phone. There were no half answers to questions or vague impressions given. He dealt with facts, exact dates and left little room for any gray area. If Sergeant Robins was an example of the department's finest, this was the place I wanted to be.

Sergeant Robins explained he was the training officer, range master and half a dozen other things for the department. And he also, as I expected, stated he had recently retired from his beloved Air Force. With instructions for the personal documents I would need and dates for testing, I ended the conversation with a new breath of life and hope. For the next few weeks, I was like a kid waiting for Christmas. I was finally going to get an honest shot at a police officer position. And having to make a trip to South Florida was a bonus!

Soon, Jack called and advised he had had a similar conversation with Robins and was pumped up even more so than I was. It was then I first asked Jack if he knew anything about this Tropical Beach area in so far as what kind of area it was or how large it was? Only being in the state a short time himself, Jack could only advise it was pretty close to him and it was located right on the beach. Jack went on to advise that all I really needed to bring clothing wise (other than some dress clothes) were swimming trunks, sunglasses and flip-flops. Considering it was the dead of winter in Armpit, Indiana, I wasted no time and immediately broke into a daily ritual of prayer and meditation asking God to please help me on this one! I promised so many things praying, I've forgotten most. I figured if God would smile just a little on me, the least I could do is help myself a little too. So for the next few weeks, I ran several times a day in preparation for the physical part of the testing and practiced taking written entry exams for law enforcement that I purchased via various publications. It was like the Blues Brothers mission from God!

It was a long twenty-one hour drive from Armpit, Indiana to South Florida and the girl I was dating at the time had never seen Florida. So it was planned, (mostly by her) that she would also go and support and cheer us on during the testing process. I stayed in regular contact with Jack in case he had heard anything that I may not have concerning the testing dates. Several times prior to leaving for Florida, the thought of not doing well with the testing and not being hired crossed my mind. The thought of spending the rest of my life in Armpit wasn't a pleasant one. Nonetheless, it might be a disappointment I would have to deal with. I really had no plan "B" to fall back on if I didn't get hired this time around and I wasn't getting any younger. These trips, mostly out of state testing for various departments took their toll on the finances. And let's face it, I would soon be thirty years old and in some instances, that's kind of late for starting a career, any career!

The time for the pilgrimage south was soon upon me. At the time, I drove a little Fiat convertible that left little space for anything but me. But this trip had to include enough clothes for me and for the girlfriend. My luggage consisted of one small paper bag. The girlfriend however schooled me on how women travel real quick. There was no negotiating or reasoning to it. This was how it is going to be and that is that. The back seat was filled along with the trunk, (all three square feet of it) with all the things that keep a female alive on the road. She even packed clothes in the glove box. Absolutely anything less would result in some sort of cataclysmic disaster. If the girlfriend and I somehow got an invitation to the Inaugural Ball, she had an outfit and matching shoes for the occasion. I would have to make do with a pair of ragged shorts and matching flip-flops.

When we arrived in South Florida, Jack and his new wife met us. Jack's wife was also from Armpit, Indiana and I had only met her briefly prior to this for just a few moments and I really didn't remember much of her. They were glad to see us and the women hit it off fairly well. The first topic and item on the agenda was shopping for the women. Jack and I however spent the first afternoon in Jack's apartment just going over the testing schedule and our strategies. But that evening, we all took a ride to scope out Tropical Beach to see what kind of place it really was. Upon entering the city limits, it appeared to be pretty much like any other South Florida city as we understood them to be. There were industrial areas, residential areas, good neighborhoods and bad neighborhoods. But most important of all, there was the beach! A large bridge spanned the Inter-coastal Waterway connecting the mainland to an island. The island was obviously a high dollar area that displayed high-rise condos, marinas, shopping plazas, restaurants and nightclubs. The beaches were of crystal white sands adorned with scantily clad young women soaking up the sun and playing volleyball. And the beach was bordered with turquoise water that stretched to the horizon. Jack and I both thought we had died and went to heaven.

Hello Men!

The following morning, Jack and I made our way to the Tropical Beach Police Department and Municipal Complex. There, we were guided to a large conference type room along with a few dozen other applicants. After mingling a few moments, we learned that most there were from areas other than the Tropical Beach area. We both found this kind of peculiar and thought that local applicants would be much better suited considering everything. But we were sure there was a reason for it and that the reason would later become apparent. As soon as the second hand of the clock on the wall struck the number 12 sharp, Sergeant Robins entered the room and introduced himself welcoming all in attendance. Anyone seating himself or herself after 8:00 o'clock sharp was the recipient of "the look" that needed no dialog attached to it from the Sergeant. As I expected, he was cheerful yet stern. He joked but was serious and most of all, he was clear in his instructions and expectations. He was truly ex-military and showed it.

The Sergeant started by putting everyone at ease. Most were and had been on edge for quite some time about the testing and rightfully so. He went on to explain that the testing would be broken up into several parts. The first phase would be the written testing followed by the background investigations. Those who made it past that portion would be asked to return at a later date and take a physical/swimming test and finally a psychological exam. I was no stranger to written exams and I was confident that there was nothing that could be dredged up in my past that would impede my chances thus far. But one never knows.

Upon completing the testing for the day, we were told that those who passed would be notified to return and to expect at least a couple of weeks to go by before we heard from the department and Sergeant Robins. Jack and I left the complex for a bite to eat and a beer to calm us. The girlfriend and I, along with Jack and his wife managed to spend another day or two enjoying what Florida had to offer before we started back to Armpit.

For the next two weeks, every time the phone rang, that reoccurring lump the size of a golf ball in my throat would appear and I would answer the phone, *Smith residence, can I help you*? I wanted to appear to be a little civilized just in case it was the department calling. The last thing I needed was for Sergeant Robins to call and I rattle off something I thought was comical. If I got hired, he'd find out soon enough how much of an idiot I really was.

As we were advised, nearly two weeks to the day had passed and I received a call from the Sergeant one evening. He started the conversation out by asking how I liked South Florida while I was down for the testing? I advised that it wasn't Indiana in the dead of winter but I would make the sacrifice and move there if I had too if I got hired. He laughed a little and then asked if I would be interested in making another trip to Florida for the remaining of the testing? I couldn't hide the relief and enthusiasm in my voice and I told the Sergeant to just give me the dates, times and location and I'd be there with bells on. He congratulated me and said he looked forward to seeing me again. I had no sooner hung up the phone and Jack called and told me he too had made the cut. For the next half hour, we were like two kids that were just told we were going to Disney World.

The second trip to Florida was reserved for a buddy of Jack's and mine named Gary. Gary required less luggage space and was a lot more laughs than the girlfriend was. And most of all, I didn't have to worry about burying my head in the sand if we went to the beach and a tanned little honey walked by. As far as the physical testing went, Jack and I were both in great shape and we were both lifeguards so the physical and swimming test was of little concern. And the physiological testing could mean a variety of things, none of which worried us either. Jack and I both had never been "formally" been committed to any psychiatric institution so that part of the testing should just be a formality we figured.

Upon arrival the second time to South Florida, Jack, our mutual friend Gary and I made the most of it immediately. Jack hadn't seen Gary for a while and didn't expect to see him again for even longer so our first night there, we hit the town in typical fashion. Unfortunately it somehow slipped our minds that Jack was now married and after staggering back to Jack's apartment in the wee hours, (completely innocent of any serious wrong doing I might add) we were cordially met at the door and reminded of the fact that Jack was now in fact very much so married! After the brawl that ensued and the dust settled, the hospitality slowly dwindled the next couple of days for Gary and I. The remainder of our stay, we were on our best behavior for Jack's sake. Jack's wife, like most other wives had a way of making her presence known even when she wasn't there. It's creepy how they do that?

The day of our second round of testing arrived and the applicants were instructed to meet under a large bridge that connected the mainland to the island. The bridge traversed about a quarter mile span of salt water that had quite a bit of large vessel traffic churning the tidal waters. Sergeant Robbins, along with his whistle and clipboard was also present and gave us instructions for our next task. "I want you to swim out to that red buoy, circle it and swim back to our present location" he barked. Well, 'that red buoy' was about a hundred yards from 'our present location' and you could visibly see the current was clipping at a pretty good rate. This might not be the walk in the park that Jack and I both expected. On top of that, we were asked to wear long pants and a t-shirt but were allowed to kick off our shoes. And there were no lifeguards or other personnel in boats in the event we ran out of steam. Apparently you were either going to make it or you wouldn't. How cool is that?

Now I can tell you first hand that salt water makes one a little more buoyant than fresh water, but long pants and a shirt in a strong current tends to negate any advantage the buoyant salt water may provide. Robbins sent us out in groups of four and Jack and I naturally took off together. Surprisingly our group had little problem with the swim. But before we made it back to land, two others in another group had to be towed back to shallow waters by fellow applicants where they could stand and walk back in. Out of about twenty or so, I think only a couple weren't up to the task and floundered. We got a brief lunch break and then we were scheduled for our psychological testing. Again, we were scheduled four at a time and went in separately for about half an hour to explain why we hated our parents or why we were afraid to touch doorknobs.

After a brief multiple-choice questionnaire and several moments of looking at a variety of inkblots, the shrink on duty sat me down and began her volley of questioning. It turns out that the regular shrink was sick that day and her Cuban secretary had been assigned to administer the "Word Association" test. Now, I've spent nearly all my life in Indiana and was not familiar with the Spanish Language one little bit. Remember this is 1980 and the only Spanish spoken in Indiana was in Spanish class at high school (of which I failed miserably) and by the migrant workers that showed up every summer to pick the vegetables. To compound matters, the secretary was chewing on a wad of gum the size of a small rat and between her accent and the gum; I had no idea what she was saying. This didn't set too well with Rosetta, (I don't know if that was her name or not) and she became very agitated thinking I was making fun of her speech when I repeatedly told her I was very sorry but couldn't understand her.

I apologized more than once for my ignorance and told her the difficulty wasn't intentional but it made no difference to her. After a few minutes and a couple more requests to repeat herself, she abruptly stopped the test and advised me that I had failed because of my attitude. I had no problem understanding that! I immediately notified Sergeant Robins and advised him of the incident and the circumstances. Sergeant Robbins knew of the psychologist's absence and also knew that the secretary was nothing more than that, a secretary and could not fail anyone. Another appointment was made the following day with someone who spoke English and I had no problems. I think that was my first stress induced gray hair!

All the testing was completed and there was nothing to do now except set back and go about our normal daily routines and wait for 'the call'. Jack continued to pump gas in Palm Beach for the rich and famous and I returned to Armpit, Indiana to formulate my next plan of attack, just in case Tropical Beach didn't pan out.

About three weeks later, I was cleaning the 'man cave' when the phone rang. Upon answering it, the familiar voice of Sergeant Robbins greeted me with a, "How cold is it up there?" I advised, "Just like it is every January, damn cold!" and he laughed. He advised that he was originally from Ohio and he knew exactly how cold 'damn cold' actually could get. He then asked if I would like to have a change of latitude and asked if I was still interested in the job. It took every bit of composure to hold back the joy and relief of hearing that! The prospect of dredging out a living in Armpit, Indiana now shifted to having a career doing something that I wanted to do and something that meant something meaningful. I swallowed hard and in a mature and composed voice I advised that I was in fact still very much interested and would gratefully accept the position. Robbins filled me in on the dates of the upcoming academy and what to expect while attending the academy. He also advised what I would need to bring and when to drop by the police station, along with the other recruits to pick up what was to be issued to us in so far as weapons, uniforms, etc. We spoke for about twenty minutes and again, as soon as I hung up the phone, Jack called and advised that he too had made "the cut" along with five others. Jack and I were like two little kids at Christmas again. We had both tried so long for a shot at what we wanted to do with our lives and finally we were given that opportunity!

For the next hour or so, we ironed out the details on me staying with Jack and his wife until I found my own place and got settled in. Finally, the sun had broken through and the usual disappointing news and fighting the 'good old boy system' was apparently over. My prayers had been answered and I had been smiled upon.

Animal House

A few days prior to the Palm Beach County Police Academy #26 commencing, all seven Tropical Beach recruits were called to the police station to meet with Sergeant Robins for our final instructions. It was here the selected seven recruits met one another for the first time as prospective coworkers. While at the police station, we drew our equipment and uniforms for the academy. The recruits consisted of Steve, Dennis, Greg, Bill, John, Scotty, Jack and yours truly. (John was soon to "wash out" of the academy.) All of us came from different parts of the country, yet in some strange bazaar way, we came together like the aligning of the planets. And from that first day; anyone with any sense at all could tell trouble was brewing on the horizon! Our instructions from Sergeant Robins consisted mainly of, "You guys represent the Tropical Police Department while attending the academy and you are expected to be on your best behavior". Robins also introduced us to our class liaison officer: Officer Jerry Ameba. This liaison officer's responsibility was to be someone who would act as a go-between for the recruits, the department and the academy.

Later, the roles of probation officer and animal trainer would be added to his duties.

The Seven bonded immediately and over the next couple of days and after several cases of beer, we grew to know each other pretty well. Greg eventually became a roommate and lifelong friend. He was a country boy through and through from Jacksonville. He was college educated and would never forgive me if I didn't mention his FSU. And like me, Greg was another who couldn't settle for any nine to five job that accomplished nothing more than supplying a means of paying the bills. Scotty was a young slender clean-cut guy that simply enjoyed life. He was bright and was more than willing to go along for the ride with about anything the Seven got into, especially after a few beers. Steve was a small stature guy that was big on everything else. He was a New Yorker that loved the outdoors and was happiest in salt-water soaked cut-offs. Dennis was from New Jersey and made sure everyone knew it. His swagger and Rocky Balboa demeanor made him stand out from the rest of us. He was another who morphed into another person altogether with a little alcohol. Then there was Bill. Bill was someone that came along once in a lifetime. There is no doubt in my mind that had Bill been born a couple hundred years earlier, he would have been the most notorious pirate in the history of the Caribbean. He soon acquired the nicknames *Jungle Cat* and *Perkins* (that was soon set aside). He was saddled with the name *Perkins* one day, when at a local fast food place, a little boy saw him at the counter and told his mother, "Look Mom! It's Perkins!" Perkins (at that time) was the chubby, bumbling sidekick of Sheriff Lobo on a television show of that era. Knowing Bill didn't much care for the less than flattering nickname. He later acquired and kept the *Jungle Cat* tag that was placed on him because of his stealth like cat reflexes under stress. In spite of all the antics and 'animal house' episodes the *Cat* was involved in, to this day he still holds the record for the highest GPA (grade point average) in the history of the police academy, an astonishing 98.8%. The *Cat* was without a doubt a scholar, a warrior, and a friend. To this day, if I had to pick one person to watch my back in a tight spot, it would be the Cat.

Before I go any further, I feel that something has to be made clear. Common sense would tell anyone that police work is inherently dangerous, very dangerous. It always has been and always will be. I think that because of this: the profession draws a certain type of individual to its ranks. From day one, it has been made perfectly clear that even when you do all the right things, your life can be taken in an instant. Anyone who wears a badge instantly becomes a target once they set foot on the streets. I don't care if you're a small town marshal or a beat cop in a large metropolitan area. Your 'time' can come from anywhere or anyone including behind a closed door, the back seat of your car, as you walk up to a home or a vehicle that you've stopped for a minor traffic violation or even as you sip your cup of morning coffee. And South Florida was no different. Tropical Beach had just lost an officer prior to our arrival. A local career punk managed to get an officer's gun from him during a disturbance call and stood over him and executed him for no other reason other than he hated cops.

Other agencies were losing officers at an alarming rate also. These officers were killed during domestic violence calls, shot while sitting in their vehicles doing paperwork, writing traffic citations, by mental health patients, and a score of other tragic circumstances. The stress was enormous and had to be dealt with in some manner. If the stress was not addressed, it would manifest itself in excessive use of force complaints from citizens, absenteeism, divorce, alcoholism, drug usage, mental health issues, and even suicide.

Remember, this was the early eighties and job stress awareness and what that stress could lead to was in its infancy. Back then, one was pretty much left on his or her own to cope with stress the best way they could. Some officers couldn't deal with it and became hard and distant and the department became their entire life. Their private vehicles often looked strangely like patrol vehicles with tinted windows equipped with large antennas. And all of their off duty time was spent with other cops resulting in no real connection with the outside world. These people always had police scanners somewhere in the background of their homes monitoring police radio traffic. And even minor things like parking violations by the public just had to be addressed whether they were on duty or off duty. In short, to these people, the world was divided into suspects and victims and if an officer couldn't create an outlet to dump the daily stress of the job, it simply ate him or her up slowly like a cancer. It may have appeared at times that the Seven were a little immature or childish and we may have been to some degree. But every one of us SLEPT LIKE BABIES at night, enjoyed life and went to work with a smile on our faces. Not many during those years in law enforcement could make that same claim!

The first day of the academy was like any other first day of school and a little awkward to say the least. The Seven scrambled for seats close to each other while still keeping in mind that it would not be wise to sit near the front for fear of being called upon regularly by instructors. But one had to always keep in mind that an attractive recruit of the opposite sex may at any moment position herself within flirting range. Some things never change.

The first task on the agenda was the introduction of the President of the Criminal Justice Department, Joseph Macy. It was the tradition for the President to welcome the new police recruits and Class #26 would be no different. Macy was a slender man and looked to be around sixty-five or seventy years old and about 6'2" inches tall with gray hair. To show that he was still in great shape and could take down anyone in the classroom, he first asked for our attention. Once he had it, without saying a word he stood behind a desk that was about waist high in front of the classroom and with his hands on his hips and standing flat footed, he made one leap upwards onto the desk with his hands remaining on his hips.

Yep, it was an attention getter all right! It not only proved that he was in great shape for an older guy, it proved that he was a little crazy too. And from that moment on, when Macy spoke, we gave him our undivided attention! Fear is a great motivator.

Our academy was a little less ridged and a little less military than most. After all, it was Palm Beach County. Class was Monday to Friday from eight to five with no uniform policy. It was more like a higher education type environment with daily hangovers. The more we got to know our assigned liaison officer, Ameba, the more we really didn't care for him. It was obvious that this position had been created just for him. No other agency had a liaison person that I knew of and we were of the opinion that he just didn't fit the mold of a "real cop" rolling his sleeves up and going in taking care of business. We were later proven right on all accounts.

Ameba was an okay guy but you had to watch that you didn't get between him and his goals of not putting a uniform on and getting in a patrol vehicle. Looking back, I think assigned to watch over the Seven was probably his darkest and most stressful days. That worked for me!

The academy was fun, interesting, scary, and intense and all we had expected. The instructors were a mixture of ex-cops, FBI, judges and educators. There were lots of classroom text materials, lectures, hands on exercises and scenarios, physical fitness, and everyone's favorite: firearms training! The recruits were put under stress, thrown curve balls regularly, and scrutinized by instructors and recruits alike. Constitutional Law, State Law, Civil Law and Supreme Court Decisions were digested like bologna sandwiches at lunch. But after business was taken care of and study materials were put away, it was time for a little R and R (rest & relaxation)!

Nearly all of the recruits were from out of state and had never seen South Florida before. If you've never been there yourself, it has a lot to offer. Our 'cultural enrichment' time was spent at the dog track, horse track, the beach, off shore fishing, nightclubs or under any convenient shade tree with a cooler or two. It was during one of these R and R evenings shortly after we had started the academy we had our first encounter with Officer Ameba. The Seven had gathered at one of the guy's newly acquired apartment for the usual cold beer break. We were all unaware his apartment just happened to be within the jurisdiction of our own Tropical Beach Police Department. As we relaxed, the beer supply dwindled and a beer run was declared. The hat was passed and a volunteer was appointed to make the run to the closest liquor store located just a few blocks away. The discussion on what brand of refreshment carried all the way to the car with still no decision on what brand of beer to buy. With money in hand, Scotty, (the designated volunteer) got behind the wheel of his black Monte Carlo and started the engine while the remaining six of us walked and kept pace with the vehicle as he pulled from the driveway trying to convince him to purchase our own favorite brand of beer. Then, unprompted and for no apparent reason, the remaining six of us leaped up on the moving vehicle: two on the hood; two on the roof; and the remaining two on the trunk. Most had an open container of beer in at least one hand. In less than a few seconds, Scotty had reached a speed where jumping off just wasn't an option and after a few blocks and a lot of laughs, the merriment abruptly ended when we heard the siren and saw the blue lights of a patrol vehicle closing in on us from the rear.

The closest place to pull Scotty's vehicle over was a convenient store/laundry mat that was located in one of the worse crime ridden sections of the city. Upon coming to a complete stop, a crowd of crack heads, drunks and derelicts started to gather around our car and the pursuing patrol vehicle. Flashing blue lights were like a magnet to the locals. Knowing we were in for a really bad experience, we braced ourselves as a really mad black patrol sergeant exited his vehicle and walked towards us. At first glance, he must have thought we were in all likelihood a group of college kids on vacation begging for a chance to go to county jail. As the sergeant chewed on us pretty good, the crowd that had gathered began to shout, "Leave them alone" and "Get out of here pig". I thought that it was rather thoughtful and nice that a bunch of strangers and derelicts would champion our cause but the sergeant was getting more and more annoyed. We finally got to the part where we were asked by the sergeant for our identification and we had to tell him that some of our I.D. was in the trunk of the vehicle "along with our weapons and leather". "Weapons!" he yelled. "Yes sir, we're in the police academy sir" I said. Astonished, he barked out, "What insane agency would hire a bunch of idiots like you?" Reluctantly I said, "Well judging from the patch on your shoulder, your department I guess"! The crowd that had gathered now resembled a prison yard of inmates and upon hearing that we were all cops (to them anyway), the crowd really started to get ugly. "They're all f---in cops" one drunk yelled.

Knowing what was inevitable, the sergeant thought it best if we all flee the scene before the rocks and bottles started to fly so he told us to get the hell out of there and the matter would be addressed in the morning. That was our first big break of our careers and a well appreciated one I might add. The following morning, Officer Ameba was at the academy to greet us before we all could stumble into the classroom. He separated us from the main body of the recruits in the courtyard and took a deep breath. I leaned to one side and whispered to my buddy Greg that this wasn't going to be pretty. Ameba started by saying that he had gotten a call from the Chief late last night who had gotten a call from the Captain who had gotten a call from the Shift Lieutenant who worked the evening shift. The Lieutenant had been advised by his road sergeant that he had observed and stopped a group of intoxicated young men riding through town draped all over a vehicle like ornaments on a Christmas tree. He went on to say that the Sergeant, upon stopping the vehicle and investigating further, learned that the drunken war party consisted entirely of recruits from our agency making a beer run. According to the Sergeant, the only reason the incident wasn't pursued further was because an angry mob had gathered to support these idiots and he thought it best to disperse before someone got hurt and the entire incident wound up highlighted on the evening news for all to see.

Ameba then looked directly at me, (we never did care for each other) and asked, "Does that sound familiar to anyone?" Like a dog that was being scolded for peeing on the floor (which I nearly did), we all hung our heads and mumbled our own little token of admittance and apologies. Ameba then advised that the matter wasn't over and that the

Seven were now on probation and was going to be watched very closely for the duration of the academy. He then told us to get into class and stormed away like we had made him look bad or something. Jungle Cat turned to the rest of the group and blurted out "Wow that has to be a record of some kind. We've been here less than a week and we're all on probation already!" After a couple high fives and some school girl giggles, we returned to class knowing that the Seven had made their mark and their presence known.

In another incident, as we were nearing the end of the academy a class picnic was planned and the Seven volunteered to supply the food and refreshments. Upon hearing this, Ameba gasped and rolled his eyes in disbelief. This had disaster written all over it. The picnic was to be at a local public park located on the beach complete with grills and open to members of the general public. Ameba had his orders to attend the function and to not let the Seven out of his sight. Rumor had it that if something went wrong; he'd probably find himself in a marked unit riding a zone like everyone else the following day.

No one really anticipated there would be no alcohol allowed at the picnic of about two hundred people. It had been a long and hard academy and a little steam had to be let off somewhere; and the Seven never did anything in a small way. It took some doing but the ribs, burgers, and oysters were abundant and something to remember. If one wanted a cold beer, the kegs were cold and plentiful. The picnic started around noon and as usual, the Cat was right on schedule and in true Cat form. From all estimates, the Cat had started his celebration around daybreak! From the beginning Ameba watched us from his lawn chair located in the shade off to one side while he sipped ice tea and we could tell he was just waiting for the axe to fall.

Some eyebrows were raised a couple of times when some clothing washed up on shore belonging to a couple female members of the party but nothing was said. The clothing belonged to dancers at a nearby entertainment place of business that had been invited and it was kind of expected. It wasn't long after that clothing from a few recruits, male and female, also started to appear. We made sure no small children were close by and kept it as discrete as we could. But regardless of what went on elsewhere in the park, Ameba would not take his eyes off of the Seven, especially the Cat! By now, the Cat was in true form and someone made the mistake of mentioning the park looked kind of like Okinawa of World War II area with the palm trees and sand. Someone even joked that the trees would be an excellent place for snipers to hide and pick off picnickers.

That's all it took to set the Cat in motion. Not wanting to lose anyone to snipers, the Cat was going to make sure all the palm trees were clear of Jap snipers! Off came the shirt, off came the shoes and away went the Cat up the closest palm tree. About ten feet from the bottom, the Cat realized that his Bermuda shorts were a hindrance to his tree climbing ability so off came the shorts leaving a white chubby guy clad in an olive green military cap with no clothes on except his banana hammock style underwear, which was also olive drab in color scampering up a palm tree like a monkey. Intoxicated or not, if the Cat said he could do or would do something, you could bank on it. Ameba eventually noticed a crowd gathering and looking up into the branches of a large palm tree and decided to investigate. As he walked closer towards the crowd, you could see his face start to distort and the look of panic set in. After an hour of convincing the Cat that the picnic area was sniper free, Ameba finally got him down and clothed. That was our last class picnic.

Looking Back

For the rest of the academy, we tried our best to keep our noses clean or at least give the appearance that we were. Once in a while, our antics from the previous evening or weekend would spill over into the following day's classroom but it would cause nothing more than a laugh or minor distraction. A laugh or minor distraction was generally a welcomed break from the seriousness of our training. The evening before St. Patrick's Day, the Seven gathered at a recruit's apartment for some cold refreshment. One thing that was learned early on was not to be the first to lose consciousness when in the company of this group. In this incident, it was Jungle Cat (who else) who passed out early. The Cat had consumed about half his body weight in beer before he even reached the apartment so he had a considerable head start. The Cat usually wore a military type olive drab cap that covered a sizeable bald spot on top of his melon head. He also sported a mustache that resembled Georgia thicket. Shortly after arriving, the Cat's head snapped back into his hibernation mode and we knew if left alone, it was there he would stay until time to get up and go to class the following morning. As usual when awoken, preparation for the day would consist of polishing off whatever beer was in his hand from the night before as breakfast and off to class he would go and grooming was something for sissies.

This was an opportunity that couldn't be passed up. Once convinced that the Cat was out for the evening, a bottle of green food color from the kitchen was dumped in his half full can of beer. After all, it was St. Patrick's Day. That just didn't seem enough so his hat was removed and everyone signed their name with a black permanent black marker on his bald spot and his hat was placed back on his head. The next morning as the recruits were getting ready for class, the Cat, who was always running behind, entered the classroom and sat down. Instantly all heads, including the instructor for that day, turned toward the Cat and marveled at his St. Patrick's Day tribute, a large bright green bush on his upper lip. Everyone just loved it. Being unaware of his St. Patrick's Day tribute, the Cat then removed his hat, which made everything perfectly clear to those who were witness to the spectacle. Sporting a bright green St. Patrick's Day mustache and a noggin that looked like a Rawlings Baseball signed by the Yankees, it was a long day for the Cat to say the least. And the remaining six of the Seven watched their backs for quite some time after that. As good of a sport as the Cat was, he wasn't one to forget soon. The rest of the academy was filled with pranks, camaraderie, and bonding. By the time graduation rolled around, we felt confident that in short order, we would be the seasoned officers that could take on the world and would be able to clean up any town and make the world safe for all.

"We're not in Kansas Toto"

In mid spring we graduated from the academy and got our instructions on whom to report to for our shift assignments and our Field Training Officer information from our respective departments. I happened to catch the evening shift and was assigned to an Officer Harrison, otherwise known as *Curly Top* on the street. The first evening was just a kind of a get-to-know-you evening. Harrison told me of what I would (in all likelihood) be seeing and doing as we listened to the radio bark out calls non-stop. What impressed me right up front was his driving ability. We were in the middle of the city on the main strip yet speed limits and signals meant absolutely nothing to this guy. Harrison drove like a mad man as I gripped the dashboard and tried to remain in my bucket seat without being thrown out the window.

As we drove, I couldn't help but notice that the area looked drastically different than the area Sergeant Robbins showed us in our tour of the city several months prior. From that tour, I remembered sandy beaches, college girls playing volleyball and beautiful condos and nightclubs. Now I was looking at abandon strip malls, half torn down fifty year old burned out buildings and shacks with numerous junk cars cluttering the weed infested and trash covered yards and streets. Harrison noticed my interest in the surroundings and asked what I was looking at. I told him that Sergeant Robbins had taken the recruits on a tour of the city several months back and I didn't recognize this part. When Harrison finally stopped laughing, he advise me that Tropical Beach was approximately 85% black (no such thing as African American back then) and was ranked fifth in the nation for violent crime per population. He also explained that the small nice area that was shown to the recruits during Sergeant Robin's tour financially supported the rest of the city that was more or less a high crime blighted area. "If Robbins showed new people what the city was really like, do you think anyone would want a job here?" he asked. Now it was clear as to why the city was hiring from outside the area! I had been "had" but good!

Harrison then advised me that the road sergeant was currently out on a call just down the road and that we were going to his location so he could introduce me to him. As we raced down the street at what seemed to be 100 mph, I prayed that no one pulled out in front of us. Just as we were arriving, Harrison said that our patrol sergeant's name was O'Reilly and that he was your "typical red headed Irishman", whatever that meant. Harrison also said that O'Reilly and a couple of other officers were out with a regular suspect who had just cut up his wife with a steak knife. That sounded pretty crucial but Harrison made it sound mundane and no big deal.

I thought all right, my first real call! As the patrol car came to a stop, I could see what appeared to be a white K-9 officer with his dog (lying asleep at his feet) and another black patrol officer casually speaking while standing alongside of the road sharing a cigarette. A few feet from them stood the sergeant. I knew him to be the sergeant from his red head of hair and the stripes on his uniform sleeve. After all, I was a trained observer now.

Harrison said, "Come on, I'll introduce you to him". As we approached, I couldn't help but notice the black gentleman O'Reilly had in what appeared to be a headlock under his left arm. As we got closer, I could see that the sergeant was administering carefully directed and spaced blows to the man's face with his free fist. In return, the man was pelting the sergeant's midsection with his fists. All this while the other two officers stood by unconcerned.

Upon seeing Harrison and I, the sergeant paused, smiled and extended his free hand for a shake. Harrison said cordially, "Serge, this is the new guy Smitty. Smitty, this is Sergeant O'Reilly" and we shook hands, all the while the black guy remained in O'Reilly's grasp flailing away. Without skipping a beat, O'Reilly said, "OK, you hit him now." Not sure of what was just requested of me, I replied, "I'm sorry?" O'Reilly said, "You hit him, I'm getting tired." I said, "Let me get this straight. You want me to hit this guy in the face because you're tired?" O'Reilly said, "Among other reasons, you got it champ!" I then turned to my training officer for an explanation and was told that we go through this every Friday evening with this guy. He gets paid and then gets drunk and assaults his wife who never presses charges. If we arrest him, he gets out in a few hours and beats her again, even worse. If he's given a dose of his own medicine, he's cool for at least a week before he beats her again. That is just the way it is." So with my training officer's blessing and my sergeant's instructions, I introduced myself to the gentleman in question with a couple of good licks. I can't tell you how awkward it felt but that's just the way it was back then and it worked.

Afterwards, the sergeant said, "You'll do just fine," and grinned. The suspect was then released and warned again that if he harmed his wife again that evening, we would be back and he would get another *warning*. He then grinned and acknowledged the advice as he had done many times prior and staggered back into the shack of a house. As we drove away from the last location, it was explained that if I ever had to take a call concerning the guy who was just given a *warning,* to be extra careful and watch his hands at all times. As casual or routine as the last encounter may have appeared to be, take nothing for granted. The gentleman who was the recipient of the *warning* had put several officers in the hospital, including a couple of sergeants over the last few years and he liked to *cut.* The actions taken by the officers had nothing to do with race or anything else. This went on between all officers and certain suspects no matter what anyone's race may have been. Generally the rule of thumb was if you have to make a trip to the E.R., your prisoner had better be laying in the bed next to you in order for you to retain your effectiveness on the streets. Before my first evening had ended, I knew I wasn't in the tropical paradise I thought I was. As a matter of fact, I was far from it! The numerous x-rays, M.R.I.'s, broken bones, and scars I have today give testimony to the accuracy of that opinion.

Race, Race and Race

Back in 1980, the country was just starting to settle down from a couple of decades of social unrest. The Vietnam War, racial tension, assassinations, women's rights and several riots nationwide were still fresh in the minds of everyone. We were still cleaning up after riots destroyed areas like Watts, Harlem, and Liberty City in Miami. The slightest spark could ignite a number of power kegs and the streets were a tense place to be at best.

No matter where one lived in the United States during the eighties, any issue or disagreement involving at least one black and one white person was immediately branded with a red-hot *racial-branding iron.* Race was the obvious or underlying reason for any issue or disagreement whether it was justified or not. It seemed no one was allowed to just "disagree". If you did disagree and you were of different color, it was racially motivated. Logic, reason, and common sense was not allowed to prevail and that is just the way it was.

Tropical Beach was no different. If anything, the city was a leader in fueling the fires of social unrest. Instead of being a leader and setting an example, racial demons flourished within the political system and local government. If you were promoted or not, it was racial; if you were disciplined or not, it was racial; if you were elected to office or not, it was racial; if you drank Coke instead of Pepsi, it was racial! Everything could be traced back to racial motivations. It got real old real quick and one learned how to play the game rather well. The only saving grace for the officers on the road was that we were so busy staying alive, the racial games that were going on around us for the most part went unnoticed. A bullet doesn't really care what color you are and one doesn't really care what color the guy is that's pulling your ass out of a jam. As for the cops, we were all one color: Police Blue!

Prior to Tropical Beach, my experience with the black culture was fairly limited. The Temptations, Earth, Wind & Fire and James Brown was pretty much the extent of my exposure. The area I had spent my last twenty years growing up and working in had only a small percentage of blacks, maybe about 20%. And outside of a rare flare up that was usually fueled by an outside organization or activist, any unrest between races was few and far between. I was exposed to blacks in high school, college, and the Marines, and we mixed on occasions but neither group went out of their way to make sure that they could verify their circle of friends included the right percentage of other races.

Nonetheless, I did have some good friends that were black. But God forbid anyone blurted out that old cliché, "Some of my best friends are black," regardless of its validity or not. That was the kiss of death in just about any social circle back then. It got so bad socially, for a while a white person almost had to carry a photo of himself hugging a black person just to prove he or she was not a card carrying "Klan's man." And even then, the black person in the photo had better be dark-skinned or it didn't count! There are still those today that profit from those old ghosts and there always will be as long as there are those who blame their shortcomings on something other than the truth. Even today, the same ones who pointed fingers three decades ago are still fueling the racial fires for self-profit and gain. One would think that we would have wised up by now and stopped listening to these morons. I hate that!

As a rookie, you are passed along to a new Field Training Officers for different phases of your training every few weeks. Officer Sammy Naska was my next field-training officer. Unique, is the only word I can conjure up to describe Sammy. Sammy was another New Yorker, from Buffalo I think. He sported a short fro haircut that was well trimmed (remember this is the early 80's), and wore dark rimmed glasses. If one didn't know, Sammy could have passed for an accountant or minister. At first glance, Sammy appeared quiet and well suited for the role of training officer. He was educated, and liked by everyone. After the first few days of mostly business, Sammy and I began to hit it off and he loosened up a bit. It was with Sammy that I first took the wheel of the patrol car and got to drive like an idiot for the first time. There's nothing quite like the feeling of being turned loose in a new high performance vehicle with a license to haul ass. I mean come on, lets be honest. That's one of the main reasons we became police officers, right?

Working with Sammy was great. For the most part, I'd drive while Sammy played his harmonica and/or spoons to the tunes on the radio. Occasionally, Sammy would ask a legal question or our current location just to see if I was paying attention, (which I always was). He also taught me how to stay alive, which I gladly passed along to my rookies when I became a field training officer. Little things like never standing directly in front of a door when you knocked and announced your presence was imbedded in our heads real quick. This practice prevented us from catching a bullet from someone on the other side of the door that didn't want to go to jail. Another tip was to park a few doors down from the actual address you were dispatched to; exiting the vehicle and easing the door closed and standing and listening before you went further. This practice ended up saving us a lot of grief later on. And the biggest tip was to never, under any circumstances back down on the streets. Once you've backed down, the word gets out pretty quick and every thug, punk, and gangster wanting to make a name for himself from that day on would try you. And that makes for a dreadfully long shift!

Driving the patrol car for the first time is definitely a benchmark in training. Another was your first dead body. Mine happen to be a natural unattended death. The call initially came out as a welfare check on someone over on the island. I had not had a death investigation yet, so Sammy asked communications to assign it to us for training purposes. The complainant was calling from New York State and had advised that his aunt had not been heard from for about two weeks and that he was concerned for her well-being. Upon arriving at the aunt's address, we noticed that the aunt's condo apartment was ground level and just a few yards from the designated parking area. As we exited the patrol vehicle, Sammy stopped and intensely looked at the apartment from the parking lot. Sammy said that these calls are no different than any other and that taking a moment to survey the scene doesn't hurt and it might be to our advantage. During training, your field training officer is God, so I too stood and just looked at the apartment. Sammy asked, "Well, what do you see?" "I don't see anything special", I said. It just looked like any condo apartment to me. Then Sammy pointed out the uncollected mail in the mailbox that was protruding and spilling out and onto the front steps and the parking space marked with the aunt's apartment number on the curb stop and the car parked in it that looked unwashed and unused. And when he told me to pay particular attention to the windowsills and what appeared to be bluish black dirt that had accumulated at the bottom of the window, I was told it was actually several thousand dead blue flies. I knew where the conversation was now heading. The final observation was when he told me to, "Take a whiff. What do you smell" Sammy asked? Only a very small sample of air had traveled up my nostrils before I caught it. It was the smell of death. Once smelled, even once in one's life, you never forget it.

The aunt had apparently passed away while lying on the living room floor watching TV with a fan on her. She had lain there for the following two weeks with no air conditioning in the middle of the South Florida summer. It was so bad; the medical examiner had to cut the carpet around her to remove the body to prevent it falling apart in their hands. Sammy and I spent nearly an entire shift inside that apartment doing the investigation. It was there on that call I learned the trick of carrying a jar of Vicks Vapor Rub in your equipment bag so you can grease up the inside of your nostrils with the menthol scent so you can tolerate the smell and do your job. And they say there's no glamour in police work.

The day finally came that every trainee waits for. At shift line-up prior to going on the road, the presiding shift sergeant was handing out zone assignments when he announced, "Smith, Zone #3." I turned to Sammy who was setting next to me, who said, "I love you sweet heart, but I'm leaving you now," which meant I was own my own and he smiled. That was the moment! All the traveling around the country taking entry tests and years of one disappointment after another was now behind me. The nepotism and academy and what seemed to be endless miles of driving and flying for interviews and written tests were a thing of the past. Despite the multitudes of hurtles and every discouraging word and obstacle that was placed in front of me, I was now a police officer and was about to go on patrol solo! I gathered my line-up notes, my hot sheet of local stolen vehicles, my brief case, and the keys to my assigned patrol vehicle and strutted towards the parking lot where my, yes MY patrol vehicle was parked. As I checked the equipment in the trunk and the interior, other officers passed by and gave me a pat on the back and wished me good luck. Wow, what a moment! I could have busted the buttons on my uniform shirt.

Well as I said, I was assigned to Zone #3 for my first shift. Zone #3 consisted of the island and it was, for the most part, the slowest zone in the city. New officers generally got Zone #3 to help break them in a little before they are thrown in the fire and are assigned a regular zone on the mainland. Nonetheless, it was my beat for the next eight hours and by God it was my responsibility and sworn duty to protect life and property. I must have driven the girls in communications nuts. If there was a person, any person, who looked at me twice, he or she got stopped and ran through the computer for warrants. I just knew there were criminals out there walking around and I just had to smoke'em out. And in between running computer checks on suspicious people, I would do traffic stops, pretty much just because I could. If others needed some radio airtime, they would just have to wait their turn. I had important work to do.

I was power mad and rapidly morphing into *Super Cop*. At the end of the shift, as I announced over the radio that I was pulling into the station's parking lot, the girls in Communications asked if I would be kind enough to step up front to the radio room to see them. It was my guess that they too wanted to wish me good luck and wanted to tell me what a fine job I was doing. After I turned in my vehicle keys and the few reports and citations I had written to the road sergeant, I marched up to Communications to see what assistance I could be them.

The door to Communications was always kept locked but for me it was opened and I was instantly invited inside. The door had no sooner clicked shut when four very unhappy women lit into me. "Do you ever take a breath or do you talk continuously," one asked. Another yelled, "I have got the worse headache from running all of your damn suspicious people and vehicle tags all shift long on the computer, I could just kill you!"

After letting her fellow radio operators' have a piece of me, the Communication Supervisor summed it up with, "Look, we have no problem with doing our jobs, but if you ever put us through another shift of this, I personally will cut your microphone cord at the dash and strangle you with it. You got it"? Head down and tail between my legs, I acknowledged the very credible threat and slowly backed out of the room. I guess that's why they call it *communications.* They were very good at it and I got the point loud and clear. And if I ever wanted to be cleared for dinner again or cleared to go off duty by communications, these were not the people to piss off. Lesson learned!

Upon arriving at home, my new roommate Greg greeted me with, "How'd it go?" Greg had been assigned to day shift and had been cleared for solo the day earlier. I simply replied, "I now know my place in the pecking order." "The girls in the radio room chewed your ass too uh?" he said. "And how!" I replied and laughed. We laughed, opened a cold beer and kicked back on our balcony, grilled some steaks and watched traffic go by on I-95 for the rest of the evening. Life was good.

The Cat Strikes

One evening after work, the Cat inhaled his usual twelve pack at one of the Seven's apartment watching Monday Night Football. Around mid-night or so, the Cat was on his way home when he caught a red light at the main intersection of town. During the week, traffic is very light and it wasn't unusual to be the only vehicle caught by the signal at this intersection during this time of the evening. The Cat had gotten into the left lane to make a left turn and was the only vehicle present. While waiting for the light to turn green, the Cat thought it was a good time to catch a few winks, you know a "Cat nap". So with his foot on the break, the Cat settled in for his snooze. On the opposite side of the intersection and directly in front of the Cat's vehicle, an oncoming vehicle with the intentions of continuing straight had stopped for their red light. Next, a vehicle on the Cat's side of the intersection pulled up on the passenger's side of the Cat's vehicle and was also waiting for the light to turn green. The driver of this vehicle noticed that the driver next to him, (the Cat) was either asleep or had suffered a debilitating medical event. The light then changed green for the Cat to turn.

All eyes turned to the vehicle that had the green but was motionless for some unknown reason. As if cued, both drivers laid on their horns in an attempt to get a reaction out of the Cat. Well they got one!

Upon hearing what appeared to be the sound of several vehicle horns bearing down on him, the Cat's head snapped forward to see two headlights directly in front of him. The Cat's first thought was that he had fallen asleep at the wheel and he was about to be involved in a head-on accident. With his catlike reflexes, the Cat threw the vehicle in reverse and floored it in an attempt to avoid a certain catastrophe. Approximately half a block behind the Cat's location was a fruit and souvenir stand that had been a landmark of sorts for several decades. An oriental couple owned the stand and had sold enough citrus's and souvenirs to tourist over the years to put two children through college. It's not really known what exactly took place next but the following day, the stand was completely gone and only a few smashed grapefruit and oranges and a couple of those little silver like sugar spoons that said "Welcome to Florida" on them littered the lot where the stand once stood. I heard later on that the oriental couple decided that it was time to retire and move back to China where it was safer.

The Cat falling asleep at red lights started to become an issue with the administration. On another one of his off days, 911 received a call one evening that there was a 'man with a gun' at a particular intersection. With not much more information than that, several cars rushed to the location not knowing what to expect. Upon arrival, we observed a vehicle stopped right where it was suppose to at a red light but the vehicle failed to move when the light turned green. With guns drawn, several officers moved up from both sides and looked into the window at the occupied driver's seat to see the Cat catching a few Z's again with his gun belt and gun next to him. I think it was that incident that prompted a probe into the Cat's drinking by the administration.

Yeah, So What?

I've always been terrible at remembering names so it took awhile to remember everyone's name when I first started work. I'd hear stories and rumors about fellow officers but I didn't know if they were exaggerations or not. Cops are the absolute worse when it comes to gossip. One of the first names I learned quickly was Officer Kenny Bosk. Word was that Kenny was a little (let's say) disturbed at times. Kenny just happened to work my shift and some of the things I noticed about him did strike me as downright spooky. Sometimes during line-up, Kenny would empty his revolver and place the bullets on his desk and talk to them. And for some unknown reason, no one in the room said anything about it. As a matter of fact, they all did their best to act like they didn't notice. Sometimes he'd stop talking as if they were speaking back to him. I never saw him smile and when spoken to, he would just grunt like a lower primate. When he walked down the halls, everyone got out of his way, even the chief. Someone told me he was involved in a bank robbery call where a fellow officer had gotten shot and killed and he was never the same after it. I stuck my foot in my mouth one day when I stepped into a local drug store and the woman from behind the counter asked if she could help me. Before I could reply, she saw my name on my uniform nametag and said, "Why you're that new guy Kenny was telling me about?" She went on to say that she had heard the department had hired several new officers and how delighted she was to meet me. The gray haired lady was very nice and a pleasure to talk to. She introduced herself as Mrs. Bosk and appeared to be older and just had that motherly demeanor and kindness to her. She eventually had to serve another customer and our conversation ended abruptly but with a smile.

At the end of the shift, while turning in my paperwork and vehicle keys, I bumped into Kenny in the hallway outside the sergeant's office door. Several other officers were also turning in their paperwork and as Kenny turned and made his way out of the sergeant's office past me, I said, "Hey Kenny. I was in the drug store over on the island today and met your mother, nice lady."

Kenny froze dead in his tracks and slowly turned his head toward me and gave me a look like an owl would give a mouse. The rest of the officers also stopped what they were doing and a couple nonchalantly slid their hands over their weapons. For nearly a minute you could hear a pin drop as we all stood frozen in time. No one moved yet no one looked directly at Kenny or me. What seemed like an eternity passed and Kenny finally turned and looked at everyone else in the room. No one wanted to make eye contact and turned their heads as if Kenny was some kind of vampire. The crowd then parted as Kenny turned and made his way to the exit and out into the parking lot. One or two officers rushed to the window and peeked around the corner to make sure Kenny was leaving and was not removing any weapons from his vehicle and returning. I then asked; "What the hell was that all about?" Someone said, "That wasn't his mother you idiot. That was his wife!" Oops… my bad! Word got out quickly of my blunder and for the next several days, other officers kept their distance from me for fear of becoming collateral damage.

On another occasion, Kenny was called to the Chief's office to receive a written reprimand for calling a citizen the dreaded "N" word. The citizen had, like nearly every other citizen, called Kenny every name imaginable during a call and Kenny had just had enough and lashed back. The citizen accomplished just what she had set out to do in provoking Kenny. She was now trying to use Kenny's blunder as a bargaining tool with the department and state attorney's office in an attempt bring race into the matter and get her case reduced or dropped altogether. This was a common ploy used by the citizens and they were good at it.

Administering discipline to Kenny was something no one looked forward to. One never knew if this was to be the amp that would finally overload Kenny's circuit box. So in the interest of fair play, those close by were warned that Kenny was coming to the station to get a "bad boy" letter from the administration and he wasn't going to be happy when he left. That gave everyone time to clear the halls and close and lock doors and make any last minute calls to loved ones. When Kenny arrived at the Chief's office, the Chief nervously shoved a "disciplinary action letter" across his desk to where Kenny was standing. Without reading it and before the Chief could get one word out of his mouth, Kenny said, "I know why I'm here. Where do I sign?" The Chief pointed to a line at the bottom of the page and Kenny promptly scribbled his signature on the sheet of paper. Kenny then made clear to the Chief, "She was a N- - - - - !" and he turned and marched out of the office leaving a very nervous and relieved Chief (who was incidentally black) wiping the perspiration from his forehead with his handkerchief.

The next few weeks, Kenny was careful to document anything, (which was nearly everything) concerning encounters with citizens that may have had racial implications. It got to the point where one evening, Kenny was chasing a suspect in his vehicle that was running on foot from a crime scene and you could tell he was being very careful to document the incident as it occurred over the radio. His radio traffic went something like:

"Headquarters, I'm chasing a black male who's on foot east bound on 31st. from Ave. S. Headquarters, he's stopped. Headquarters, he's picking up a brick. Headquarters, he's going to throw the brick. Headquarters, he's thrown the brick. Headquarters, I've got a smashed windshield. Headquarters, I'm going to arrest him now."

The road sergeant at the time finally got with Kenny and convinced him it wasn't necessary to give a blow-by-blow account of his actions in order to keep the brass off his tail. Kenny was unique in his own special way, but there was one thing that was certain. As frightened as his fellow officers were of him, so was the general public. So if the crap hit the fan and Kenny showed up as your back up officer on your call, you could count your back being covered!

The Monkey Poster

Racism is a two way street. For those on the same level, such as patrol officer to patrol officer, there were practically no racial problems in those days between us. We were too busy watching out for each other and staying alive. But as you advance through the ranks and reach a certain level, you now had time on your hands to get caught up in racial issues and any political controversies. And if there weren't any, you could always create something that would benefit your agenda with just a little effort.

A black Lieutenant that no one really cared for (I'll call him Charlie B) had no sooner been promoted to the rank of Captain when for no reason other than because he could, he disregarded the seniority rule and took every black officer off of night shift and replaced them with white officers. It made no matter if the shift change created enormous family hardships or not. One could plead their case but he would just smile and tell you that's just the way it is. I can tell you first hand, night shift can get old pretty quick.

As it happens, one morning on duty, about 4 a.m., as I was reading the Sunday News Paper in my patrol vehicle, I turned the page to see a full-page ad that a local car dealer had placed. The ad was a large color photo of what appeared to be a family of chimpanzees. There was Papa, Mama and two little ones and all were dressed in their Sunday best and embracing in a group hug.

It was a comical photo and obviously not printed with any racial intent, unless that is of course you made it racial. It was simply a funny picture for God's sake! Thinking that the rest of the shift could use a laugh from being jammed on the night shift, I cut the photo from the paper and wrote below the caption, 'Officer of the Month, Captain Charlie B., Family Man.' I then stopped by the station and posted it on the line-up bulletin board. Along with *my* cartoon were at least half a dozen other comic clips and cartoons of fellow officers, local judges, state attorneys, and defense lawyers that various other officers had pinned up for a laugh. Every one of them, to any sane person, was obviously not posted with any malice but to simply poke fun at someone or to generate a smile from the troops. Everyone was fair game or so I thought!

Oh my God, the firestorm that followed was cataclysmic. One would have thought that someone had cut the Pope's throat and nailed his lifeless body to the bulletin board. The following morning, the night shift had been cleared for relief and most had gone home for the day. But as the day shift arrived, hoots and howls filled the halls and offices of the station. From the administrative offices all the way to the custodians office, people were falling all over each other because of the "monkey poster" that was posted in the line-up room. And it wasn't so much the poster as to whom it targeted. Who in the world had the balls enough to lock horns with Charlie "B"? Captain Charlie "B" didn't just go after white officers; he appeared to have a chip on his shoulder for everyone, except the young female employees, but that's another story. Few held him in high regard and everyone held his or her breath as Charlie "B" entered the station that morning. It was obvious that something was going on that involved him, but he couldn't quite figure out what it was. I don't know who spilled the beans, but when Charlie "B" finally found himself standing in front of the bulletin board in the line-up room staring at the poster, someone said his jaws tightened and he clenched his fists. One account from a sergeant who was present and witnessed the spectacle, said Charlie "B"s face distorted and then he grinned a devilish grin that even frightened him as he pealed the poster from the wall using the tips of his fingers being careful not to touch the cartoon itself. He then walked it up to the detective division and laid it on the table of Detective Larry Jersey who was our best crime scene fingerprint guy and told him that he wanted to know whose prints were on the poster by lunch. Jersey later told me it took all he had to keep from busting out laughing when he saw it.

He also said that he wasn't thrilled about spending the rest of the day doing the Captain's grudge investigation. So to save time, he placed the officer's print cards in "order of probability" of who he thought might have pulled the prank. He said he placed my card on top of the stack and it was first to be compared to the prints on the cartoon. I took it as kind of a compliment. In any case, Jersey gave the Captain a nod and a 'yes sir' and proceeded to pull the fingerprint cards of the officers from the filing cabinet.

By now, I was home and asleep safe and sound in my own little bed. Around noon, my roommate came into my room and shook me until my eyes opened and I was looking at him nose to nose. "Smitty, tell me it wasn't you," he said over and over. "What the hell are you talking about?" I asked. "There's a notice on the bulletin board stating 'person or persons responsible for posting the prejudicial poster on the line-up room bulletin board will be immediately

terminated when located. It was place there by the Chief."
"Are you kidding me, prejudicial?" I asked.

"The Captain demanded that the Chief fire whoever put it there and the whole station has been upside down over it all morning. Everyone thinks it is great that someone poked a little fun at Charlie "B," but Charlie "B" is making it a racial issue." he said.

I immediately got up and called the station and asked for the Chief hoping he would accept my apology and explanation that it was just a joke. "Chief, it was me who placed the cartoon on the bulletin board, but there was absolutely no racial intent." I explained. The Chief kept it short and sweet. "Be in my office at 2pm." he said.

Well I knew it wasn't going to be pleasant, but I never expected what was waiting for me. As I entered the Chief's office, the chief and a Captain (not Charlie "B") along with a tape recorder was ready for my confessional. Just in case things turned ugly, I brought along my union representative to be present which never hurts. In police work, everyone makes mistakes from time to time. And when questioned about anything, the number one cardinal rule is to tell the truth, and nothing but the truth. A half-truth is a lie and will get you fired on the spot. I had nothing to lie about so the entire incident was regurgitated step by step.

After a reenactment of the crime of the century, another twenty minutes or so was spent apologizing and groveling (which I can do very well). I also begged for mercy for any misunderstandings or hard feelings I may have caused and admitted that staff officers should remain 'off limits' to pranks from line-personnel. As I left the Chief's office hanging on to what ass I had left, my union representative remained behind to await the decision from the Chief as to my fate. A short time later, my union representative exited the Chief's office. "What's the verdict?" I asked quickly. "He wants to fire you," he said. But before I fainted right there in front of him and the Chief's secretary, he smiled and said, "We, (the union) met him half way and you got two weeks off without pay."

Me prejudice, I thought to myself. It made no difference at all that I had headed up several fundraisers for black members of the community nor did it matter that I had organized a charity event for a black officer that had been seriously injured in a motorcycle accident on duty netting the officer a $10K check, (that I never even got a thank you for I might add). I had even been a member of the "Big Brothers" organization with my 'little brother' being a young black child. I didn't recall any black officers doing any of these type things for their own community. But none of that came into play. For the sake of convenience and justification, my prank was branded prejudicial, case closed. Charlie "B" however was allowed to carry on for years in his anti white officer campaign. That sucked but everyone knew the truth and that's all that mattered I guess.

As soon as we rounded the corner and started down the stairs, the representative made sure no one was listening and started laughing and said, "Smitty, you are the man of the hour and our hero. No one has ever stood up to Charlie "B" until now and everyone was going to call in sick tomorrow if something happened to you. But to play it on the safe side, try and stay out of the spot light for a while, okay?"

So for the next couple of weeks, a friend of mine who managed a hotel on the beach hired me as a cabana boy/custodian at the Hilton Inn just to keep me busy and earn a few bucks, some sacrifice there. When I returned to work with a nice tan after my two weeks of exile, I was greeted like a soldier returning home from the front by the night shift. The story of the "monkey poster" still brings a laugh to those who remember it, everyone except me that is.

Another prank that nearly cost me more than my job was the funeral home prank. All alarm calls warrant at least two officers to respond. The first to arrive is usually designated as the primary and the second is the back up. One hot Sunday afternoon, an alarm call came in indicating that the perimeter of a local funeral home had been breached. And as usual, a zone vehicle and myself were given the call. I was just around the corner so I arrived within seconds. Upon observing the front door of the funeral home, it was obvious that someone had not closed the door tight when they left work and possibly when the air conditioning kicked on, it forced the door open enough to set the alarm off.

Officer Spicer, who was my back up, was relatively new to the force and a very low-key individual. He was bright and one of my better officers. Officer Spicer was also a black officer who got shook pretty easily when it came to things like snakes, ghosts or the devil. As a result, he'd probably be the last one to play a practical joke on while investigating a call at a funeral home. So when I heard his voice falter a little when he confirmed that he too was also in route to the funeral home, I just couldn't pass it up.

Knowing I had a few minutes before Officer Spicer arrived, I searched each room looking for the perfect dark corner or crevasse to hide in. As I reached the rear of the building, I entered what appeared to be the preparation room where the bodies were embalmed and was a bit uneased to find their current customer stretched out on a table. He was a white male in his late seventies or early eighties and was covered to his chest with a white sheet. It looked like someone had been putting make up on him in preparation for his burial service and had dropped everything at quitting time. Next to him was an empty gurney with a sheet that someone was kind enough to leave out for me.

This was too good even to be planned in advanced. I picked up a nearby phone and called dispatch and told them that I was turning my radio off and advised that the alarm was false and not to be alarmed if they didn't hear me on the air for the next few minutes. Because they knew me well and how Officer Spicer was, they put two and two together and simply asked me to, "Take it easy on the poor guy will you."

I chuckled and hoisted myself up on the gurney and as I was covering myself up with the sheet, I could hear Office Spicer advise dispatch over the radio he too had arrived and was entering the building. I then turned my radio off and positioned the gurney as to block anyone from passing through the room without first having to move the gurney to one side. I then pulled the sheet up and over my head and I took a deep breath and waited in the darken room.

In the following moments I could hear movement in the adjoining rooms and could hear Officer Spicer whisper, "Sgt. Smith, Sgt. Smith, please don't do it, please don't," as he worked his way closer to me. It took everything I had to hold it in. Finally, I could hear his footsteps shuffling through the room I was in and when he caught sight of the elderly man stretched out on the table next to me, I could hear him gasp and say, "Oh Lord! Oh Lord!" and I knew he would assume that I was just another customer under the sheet waiting my turn to be spruced up. When I saw his flashlight through the sheet and felt his body brush against the gurney I was laying on, I knew it was time.

What I didn't know was Officer Spicer had his flashlight in one hand and his duty gun pulled and at the ready in his other. As he walked by the gurney I was laying on, I eased my hand out from under the sheet and grabbed his duty belt and held on. When he felt the resistance, he assumed he had snagged his duty belt on something and turned to free it.

When he turned, he saw what he thought was a dead person not only setting up before his eyes but this dead person had him in his grasp and wasn't letting go. When I sat up, the sheet slowly slid from my face and I could see Spicer's face and immediately realized that I was about to meet my maker if I didn't do something quick. Spicer was raising his weapon and shaking so bad, I could hear the loose change in his pocket jingle. I shouted several times, "Easy, easy, it's me. Take it easy." It took a few moments for Spicer (and me) to regain our breath and compose ourselves. Afterwards, I wondered which one of us got the crap scared out of them more: him or me. Yes, he was really pissed for a while but come on, what are friends for?

Sergeant Argust

Over the course of time, a patrol officer will in all likelihood have several supervisors to work under. My favorite was Sergeant Norm Argust. The local female population affectionately referred him to as the *Silver Fox*. His hair was as silver as any and he was always quick with a smile. To many of us, he was the textbook sergeant. He appeared on every call he was close to, but never interfered with the officers and let the officers handle the call their own particular way. I can still see him with his arms folded, standing in the background in case you needed him for any advise, questions, or backup. He was truly a gentleman and a professional and someone who could be approached any time for any reason.

When I first started with the department, like many others, I hadn't established much credit being from out of state and finances were a little slim. One day, while on duty, I was asked to come to the station where I was instructed to call back home to Armpit, Indiana. I knew it was bad news from the way they acted. Upon doing so, I learned that two members of my family had been killed in an auto accident and I needed to return to Indiana a.s.a.p. I could have driven but it would have taken a full day and I needed to get there as soon as I could but I didn't have the money to fly. Upon learning what had happen and realizing the urgency of getting home fast, Sergeant Argust took me to one side and handed me a credit card in his name and simply said, pay me back when you can. I'll never forget the kindness he showed.

When I returned from Indiana, I went straight back to work. Within a few nights, we were dispatched to an all night restaurant called The Clock in regards to a disturbance. It was your typical greasy spoon place that catered to the port workers and the late night drunks and prostitutes. It was common to get calls from The Clock, especially after midnight, requesting patrons be removed from the premises for a variety of reasons.

The girls at The Clock treated the officers really well and they were always glad to see us come in for our coffee breaks. On this early morning, we received a call from The Clock advising that a drunk was wrecking the place and needed to be removed. Two zone officers, a K-9, and myself, along with Sergeant Argust, got the call. We all pretty much arrived together and I was the first through the front doors of the business. It wasn't necessary but a waitress immediately pointed to a table near the middle of the establishment where a large man around thirty years old was sitting alone. The man had obviously been drinking and was yelling at the customers sitting next to him for no apparent reason. I also noticed that positioned above the drunk was a large ceiling fan that appeared to be turned on high in an attempt to circulate the air and cool the room a bit.

Upon observing the other officers and I walked in his direction, the drunk reached in front of his plate of scrambled eggs and grabbed the mustard and ketchup containers firmly in both hands. Not bothering to even lift them from the table, he squeezed until they were empty sending the colorful condiments upward and into the blades of the ceiling fan where it was promptly distributed outward for about ten to fifteen feet. I instantly recalled when I was a kid, I remembered going to the local county fair and for twenty five cents, a carnival worker would attach a piece of paper to rapidly rotating disk in an enclosed container. While it spun, you could squirt different colored paint onto the paper and centrifugal force did the rest. The result was a kind of pretty multi-color piece of "spin-art" that was placed in a paper frame when you were done. As the room quickly became such a piece of "spin-art" from the yellow and red condiment, we confronted the drunk at his table as Sergeant Argust remained watchful near the front door next to the cash register with his arms folded as usual letting us do our jobs.

The drunken man rose to his feet and a confrontation immediately erupted. If the confrontation had just remained verbal, the drunk would have just be removed from the business and sent on his way. But as we reached the cash register where Sergeant Argust was standing, the man suddenly clenched his fist, turned and threw a wild punch in the direction of the K-9 officer walking behind him. K-9 Officer David Kissman, nightstick in hand, (which was normal) was ready for such an attack. As the punch blew by Dave's face, Dave countered with a two handed Louisville Slugger type swing which caught the drunk in the lower back area and sent him crashing forward and downward in an uncontrolled crash and burn type dive reminiscent of a Japanese Zero being blown out of the sky at the battle of Midway.

As the floor of the restaurant rushed upwards to greet the belligerent drunk, he desperately tried to grasp anything he could in an attempt to avoid the inevitable crash. In doing so, his right hand somehow found the glass penny gumball machine that was standing next to the cash register sending it to the floor ahead of him. Upon shattering, hundreds if not thousands of colored gumballs shot in all directions. It looked like a super nova of color. The left hand of the drunk however managed to catch the left front pocket of the sergeant's trousers that he held on to until he hit the floor pulling the sergeant's now detached pants leg down to his ankle. The sergeant, not flinching an inch during all of this was now standing, arms still folded, while his white with red polka dot boxers blew in the breeze for everyone to admire. It was indeed a Kodak moment! Calmly, Sergeant Argust bent over, pried the fingers of the drunk off of his pant leg that was now bunched up like an accordion around his ankle, pulled the pant leg back up and held on to it as he exited the restaurant and drove away without a word like it was just another day at the shop.

Later, while at the station and during the drunk's booking for disorderly intoxication and assault; it came time to fingerprint him and have him sign his paperwork. He had calmed down considerably by then, but just in case, Dave and his stick stood by to assist. Upon releasing him from his cell, the now semi-sober man exited the cell and smiled. He then did a few jumping jacks and touched his toes a few times for good measure. Dave and I were a bit baffled over the behavior and asked what the deal was? The man went on to explain that he had had a bad back for several years and had undergone several unsuccessful surgeries and treatments in an attempt to get even the slightest relief from the pain. But now, for some unknown reason, his back felt like new and there wasn't even the slightest discomfort. The prisoner shook Dave's hand nearly off and couldn't thank the both of us enough. According to him, it was nothing less than a miracle. From that moment on, K-9 Officer Dave Kissman was known and referred to as Dr. Kissman by his fellow colleagues.

Josh

At one time in my career, I found myself setting on a review board with several other people who's job it was to screen new applicants for law-enforcement. Applicants would come in all cleaned up with their best face on, dressed well and sit at the end of a long table in some conference room while board members asked a series of questions of the applicant in an attempt to gain some insight on their characters. The questions would usually be the old standard questions like, "Tell me why you would like to get into law-enforcement Mr. Jones." And then the applicant would put on their sincere face and give the old generic answer about how much they wanted to help their community and be a part of something worthwhile. And upon hearing the answer, the board members would smile and nod their "bobble heads" in approval similar to the pat on the head a dog would get for fetching a stick.

Well to me, it was all "bull" with a capital "B"! I can't tell you how many times these idiots would get hired and for the rest of their careers, it was all about them. Unless there was overtime pay involved, these guys (and gals) could care less about their 'fellow man or the community'. So when it came to my turn to ask the applicant questions, I only had two. They were;

What was the last thing in your life that you did, at work or privately that you are really proud of?

And just how long ago was that?

Most of the time there was just silence and other times you could see the panic set in. But at least it gave you some serious insight on the applicants and their sincerity.

Well, I would forget that sometimes these applicants were 'favorites' of someone upstairs or were shoe-ins and the screening board was just a formality. And when my questions brought out their true colors, it made some people very uncomfortable. So my tenure on the review board was short lived. Simply put, I wouldn't play ball and issue a pass to just anyone.

As life and my career went by, I found myself utilizing different methods to measure the passing of time. The first couple of decades of my life were measured like most others, with days, months and years on a calendar. But during my law-enforcement career, I started to use things like memorable events or certain benchmarks in my life. And these points in time were generally very good times that added to my growth and development as a person or officer or were very bad times that contributed another nail in the coffin. As a rule, everyone has their own share of bad times and they don't really care to hear about other's bad fortune. That is unless you're one of those who wallow in misery like a pig in a mud hole. And we all know at least a few of those people who just can't seem to find anything else to talk about except how bad they have it and how miserable they are. What I would like to share now is a point in time in my career where something was added to my definition of the word 'love'. Not many in law-enforcement can relate or connect the word 'love' to their law-enforcement job description. Maybe I was just lucky?

The Westside Grill was a neighborhood watering hole and restaurant that claimed a fair portion of my paycheck for several years, and for good reason. The food was good; I knew nearly everyone and I just felt comfortable there. The owners were great people and were very active in local charities and supporting the community. This also attracted a certain type of character or clientele. I knew one of these people as Mr. Bill. I'm sure Mr. Bill had a first and last name like most, but I never was privy to them for some reason even though we were somewhat friends. He let it be known that his profession was "Communications Consultant", but I later found out that he just owned a bunch of two-way radios and was also good at repairing them. He also worked as a security guard from time to time, which kind of came in handy when you have a bunch of walkie-talkies lying around. He was a slender salt and pepper haired guy that seemed to be trapped in the seventies. His bell-bottoms and short Afro supported the seventies description well. Mr. Bill was always teeming with stories of working security at races, county fairs, concerts and charities. But most of all, Mr. Bill was a genuinely nice guy in my book. And on several occasions, Bill, (if you're a friend you can call him Bill) would extend an invitation to work an event with him and his crew; which were also in most cases Westside patrons. The events were generally on weekends and involved a free stay and meals at a hotel near by the event. And the number in the crew varied from just Bill and another to nearly a dozen or so depending on the event.

One evening after my shift, during a cheese burger and a large order of house fries, Bill appeared at the Westside and was instantly invited to my table for some conversation and dinner. As usual, Bill was gearing up for an upcoming event and was excited about the quality of the hotel that was booked and the great crew he had to work with him. And as usual, he extended an invitation to me. I think most people would find an invitation to work as security at an event like a Grand Prix Race in Miami or at a rock concert that headlined a big time rock star exciting or just plain fun. But after a couple dozen years working as a police officer, doing the security guard thing would be more like putting in some overtime. But for some reason that I still haven't put my finger on, something told me to say yes this time, so I did.

Bill was a little taken back by my acceptance of his invitation and even more so excited. So Bill began to spill out the details of the event while we ate. As he advised me of the dates of the event and name of the hotel we were staying at, my thoughts turned to rubbing elbows with some music celebrity or hanging around the pits shooting the breeze with some Formula One or NASCAR driver. Who knows, I might even get an invitation to a party after the race or concert? That would be great!

After Bill advised that the event was being held at an outdoor arena in Miami known for hosting track and field events and that the participants would be from all over the Southeastern United States, Bill finally made it clear that the event was the Special Olympics. Frankly I was a little disappointed and it kind of caught me off guard for a moment. I knew that the Special Olympics involved handicapped people, generally youth that suffered from disabilities ranging from mental retardation to genetic impairments. I also knew from seeing portions of other Special Olympics on the television that it wasn't going to be a picnic of any sorts working it. And I could forget about hob-knobbing with the rich and famous right now.

It was about this time that I started to really feel ashamed of myself. Everything conveyed to me by Bill up to this point indicated that a charity may be involved, yet I fooled myself into thinking it was a glamour event where the proceeds went to a charity. I didn't know how I would feel being around hundreds of physically and mentally challenged people; it honestly gave me a case of the "willies". The only exposure I had had up to that point with this group of people was when I was younger and around my best friend's little brother who was born mentally retarded. And all I knew about him was you had to watch him like a hawk for fear of doing almost anything. In short, I was about as ignorant as one could get about a subject that was about to swallow me alive.

As the days went by and the event grew closer, I spoke to Bill a number of times kind of hoping that the Olympics had been moved or canceled for some reason. Bill also gave me my assignment along with the other members of the group who met one evening at the Westside. The assignments ranged from parking detail, lost and found, security for the office, and crowd control in front of the grandstand to even officiating the event. One assignment for the officials was labeled "official hugger". This was the official who was waiting just over the finish line with their arms extended outward and ready to give the participant a *big hug* just for finishing the race. All participants got their hugs, win or lose!

My ignorant and shameful hand went up immediately requesting crowd control in front of the grandstands. The thought of having a sweaty mentally retarded person wrapped around me like a wet bath towel just didn't appeal to me. It was a selfless request that would have turned my mother's head in disgust. Nonetheless, I was now designated as crowd control. Bill then handed out the radios (his favorite part) and designated our call signals. Mine was "Grandstand 4" if I remember correctly. After some more insight and instructions on the best route to the hotel, we disbanded and went our separate ways for a good night sleep.

Upon arriving at the hotel in Miami the following day, I immediately checked into the hotel and took a look at the room that I was sharing with whom else, Bill. Bill was kind enough to keep my bed clear of his debris but the rest of the room looked like a relief center for some natural disaster. Orange traffic cones and vests, yellow *DO NOT CROSS THIS LINE* tape, road flares, batteries of all sorts and sizes, chargers, first-aid kits, headsets, binoculars, bottled water, power bars, first aid kits and of course lots and lots of radios! As a police officer, I had once worked a sizeable train wreck involving several vehicles and multiple injuries and didn't have nearly the equipment that Bill had laid out for the next couple of days. It was obvious that for the next two days, Bill was in his element and was indeed "the man"!

The day of the event, we all gathered around noon and took two vans to the event site called Tropical Park to familiarize ourselves with the layout. It was an older facility that had seen its share of events over the decades and what it lost in newness it made up for with history and nostalgia. It appeared that its original function or purpose was track and field events. Palm trees and flowers adorned the huge parking area that flowed into the stadium. The well-lit grandstand spanned the length of the track area from end to end. I estimated seating to be about ten thousand or so. Under the stadium seats were the concessions, offices, and rest rooms. As Bill walked us to our stations explaining what to do in the event of a variety of emergencies, I caught my first glimpse of some of the participants who had also showed up early to practice or sight see.

It was about this time that the world, like an image in the eyepiece of a telescope began to come into focus. It was now obvious who the participants were to be. And each had at least one other person supporting them (physically or motivationally) to assist them in any way they could. There were male and females, young and old with disabilities ranging from mild to devastating impairments. And to some, their means of locomotion was just their sheer determination that allowed them to do nothing more than simply place one foot in front of the other. Some were even assisted by mechanical means. And then there were those who brought them there. Parents, siblings, church groups and sponsors alike were in the wings keeping a watchful eye on their athlete. It was something to behold and think about for the rest of the evening at the hotel. And believe me, I did. I can't remember a day when I gave thanks so many times for my good health as well as for my family's and friends. I even thanked God for my healthy pets at home. For some reason, I just couldn't give enough thanks.

For me, five o'clock in the morning is usually reserved for fishing or hunting. But today, it was show time. A hearty breakfast in the hotel dining area and a last minute briefing was all there was time for. As we walked through the hotel parking lot to the vans that were parked in the front of the hotel, I couldn't help but notice what a beautiful South Florida day it was. But it was still South Florida, so the twenty-minute ride to Tropical Park was like the usual cheap carnival roller coaster ride with the occasional "Move over! & You jerk!" honk from another motorists and a polite 'No thank you,' to the homeless guy wanting to wash your windshield at the intersection for a buck. If I had any thoughts of ducking out, it was too late now. I had my official orange "staff" ball cap and tee shirt on, my instructions in my pocket, and most of all, I had my fully charged assigned radio from Bill.

Even as early as we were, there were plenty who had arrived before us. As I stepped from the van and started to amble toward my assigned area, I surveyed the stadium and its occupants along the way. It was at about this point in time when I stopped referring to the participants as participants and started to call them what they really were: "athletes".

Sports has always played a big role in my life and has consumed a lot of my free time. I was always involved in some kind of sport at school and growing up meant baseball, softball, bowling, golf, snow and water skiing, or anything else I could break a good sweat or bone at. I even coached and trained Olympic Amateur Boxers for several years, so my knowledge of what it took to be referred to as an "athlete" was genuine. I also never had a father and sports seemed to fulfill that testosterone driven urge nearly all healthy young males have throughout their lives. So I think I'm qualified to entitle one with the label of athlete when I see one.

These were obviously not people who had nothing to do that weekend and thought they would come out and kill a few hours running around a sports arena. What I saw in their faces was extreme focus and a level of desire and determination to win. The level I saw exceeded even those who competed in professional sports. These athletes weren't competing for an opportunity to make a lot of money and be famous. There were no television cameras or commercial contracts awaiting the winners of the individual events here. These athletes were simply here to prove something to them selves. And they meant business!

The time had come for the games to begin. The opening ceremonies consisted of the traditional lighting of the Olympic Torch and then all the local dignitaries and politicians had to make their speeches about how important the games were and how everyone should support them. Then they all disappeared not to be seen again. I was located right in front of the grandstand that was nearly filled to capacity. Just behind me was a staging area that was designated for the athletes to warm up in and await their particular event. That is where I first came into contact with Josh.

Just a few feet behind me and just on the other side of a chain link fence stood a woman. Utilizing my years of investigative skills and powers of observation, I surmised from her clothing, speech and the way she carried herself that she was (let's say) "well off". The words she spoke were educated and cultured. And the terms well bread and aristocrat also came to mind while observing her. There was little doubt the wide rimmed sunbonnet and pearls she wore weren't purchased at the local Wal-Mart, and next to her stood a young boy about eleven or twelve years of age. His light yellow hair was cut very neatly and he was spotlessly clean, almost "spooky clean" for someone his age. He wore a pair of green silk-like gym trunks and a yellow sports tank top with a number "5" on the front. And like every other contestant; on his back in bold letters safety pinned securely was his name. On his was the name "Josh".

An hour or so went by and several events and awards were given out yet Josh and his patient mother hardly flinched let alone warmed up for Josh's event. My guess was she just had the Mercedes-Benz detailed and didn't want it soiled with a sweaty kid. They could have sat down on the dusty bleachers just a couple feet behind them, but she chose to stand and occasionally wipe what perspiration there was from her and her son's face with the white laced handkerchief she clutched in her free hand.

As the day progressed, I spent my time enjoying the competition and listening to Bill on the radio in his height of glory keeping the arena free of crime and organizing traffic flow in the parking area. Obviously considering the event, there was also more than the normal amount of lost kids that needed their parents located too. And again, Bill was your man!

As the current event was grinding down, the announcer came over the loud speaker and announced that the participants of the 'eight eighty relay' should start heading toward the staging area. The eight eighty relay, for those who may not be familiar with track and field, is a race of 880 yards with teams of four runners in each team. Each runner runs 220 yards and passes a baton off to the next runner with the last runner being called the anchor. There are usually four teams or more in each race. This had to be one of the most grueling events on the agenda for these athletes. For an average person, grasping a moving piece of pipe called the baton and sprinting two hundred and twenty yards and passing it off to another runner without dropping it is a feat in its own and is usually measured in hundredth of seconds. In this case, because of the disabilities and condition of the runners, the unit of measurement was likely to be just minutes and seconds. Even to finish such a contest would be a major accomplishment for some of these athletes under the circumstances they were dealing with.

As with all the events prior to this, I paid particular attention to the crowd in the grandstands. The applause given to the athletes was not for their athletic accomplishments, but rather for their perseverance and sportsman like conduct. Just about any healthy person could jump higher or run faster than these youngsters. This was about something else and it truly was their day in the sun.

As Josh's mother escorted him toward the starting line where he would be turned over to an official, I took notice of the impairment Josh was dealing with. Along with what appeared to be a mild mental retardation, his right leg and foot bent inward, something I hadn't noticed while they stood behind me. This caused him to take about three steps to everyone his mother took. Along with his right leg, he held his right arm close to his side and his hand was clenched in the typical fashion that comes with muscle paralysis common with cerebral palsy. Josh struggled to even walk, let alone run. I wondered how in the world is this brave little guy was going to do this? But he was just one of many who took on the challenge.

Upon turning Josh over to an official, the mother came back to where I was standing. And to my surprise, she struck up a conversation about how beautiful the day was. I could tell she wasn't really concerned about the weather but just wanted to get her mind off being there. We talked for a few moments and I could tell she was a loving mother. Yet she spoke of Josh as if he was a very small child and it was obvious she was very protective. It had sounded like Josh had been raised like one would keep a fragile heirloom, sheltered and away from all bad things. I tried to assure her that everything would be just fine but I could tell my efforts were in vain. As the contestants from the previous event got their hugs and awards and turned over to their parents or other loved ones, the new contestants took their places on the track. I had no way of knowing what was about to happen and how it would dramatically affect every person in the stadium including myself.

As the mother and I stood off to one side near the sidelines, I noticed that Josh was placed at the far end of the circular track, which indicated to me that he was the designated anchor for the team. It was his job to take the baton and run the last leg of the race for his team. It was the most important position on a relay team for most races are won or lost by this person. After the athletes were introduced by name, they gave their traditional wave to the crowd. The contestants then took their positions. The smiles of the competing athletes were now gone and were replaced by looks of determination and focus. The running shoes were cleaned of debris and muscles were stretched and shook out like one would shake out a dirty rug. The lead off runners took their places in the starting blocks and the official's hand was raised and the starting pistol was fired and the race was officially on.

In any other race similar to this one, the focus would normally be on speed. But as I mentioned before, the focus on these athletes was their determination! Each runner had his or her own distinctive means of locomotion. And each had adapted in some manner to overcome their particular handicap. But the lack of speed was made up for with courage, and the cheering spectators knew it and supported their favorites.

What seemed like several minutes passed and the race was pretty even to this point. As the third runner rounded their turn in the track and reached outward with baton in hand, the anchor runner began to move forward anticipating the handoff. I turned to Josh's mother to give her some encouragement only to see her preoccupied with reading what appeared to be a brochure or itinerary of some sort. I wasn't really surprised to see that her interest in Josh's efforts went somewhat unnoticed. None-the-less, Josh was giving it everything he had on the track. As the runners rounded the turn and started to pass in front of where we stood, Josh was just barely in front of the pack of runners. Then it happened!

Josh noticed that his mother who was standing to my side was not watching the race and observing his efforts. Upon seeing this, Josh stopped dead in his tracks, craned his neck for a better look and started to wave the hand that carried the red baton shouting, "Mom, Mom look!" This went on for several seconds. At first, the crowd didn't realize what was happening, but quickly they put it together and the laughter started. Nearly everyone pointed and laughed at the lanky young man who couldn't care less about the race and only wanted his mother's attention and approval. At first, Josh's mother was embarrassed and attempted to hide her face by lowering the brim on her bonnet and stepping a bit behind me. But Josh was having no part of it and kept waving for his Mom to give her recognition. Realizing that Josh wasn't about to move until she gave him her undivided attention she answered his shouts with a wave and put aside her vanity and embarrassment long enough to stand tall and yelled back at her son, "I see you Josh, I see you son!"

By now, the rest of the runners were what appeared to be an insurmountable distance from Josh and nearing the finish line. But Josh now had his mother's attention and something to prove. From this point on to this day, I'm not sure what really took place. But I know what I saw. And to call it anything less than a miracle wouldn't be accurate or fair.

When Josh again faced forward and in the direction of the finish line, something happened to his twisted little frame that enabled him to explode into a sprint that instantly silenced all in the grand stand who were laughing and pointing at him. No one could believe what they were seeing. The dead silence lasted for only a few seconds and as Josh quickly closed the remaining gap between himself and the rest of the competition, the once 'less than sympathetic' crowd were now on their feet and cheering like nothing I've ever witnessed. I turned a bit to see if Josh's mother was witness to what was happening and upon seeing her face and the tears streaming down her cheek; it became crystal clear to me what was occurring.

Since the birth of Josh, his mother had struggled

to cope with all that came with being the parent of a handicapped child. The acceptance of having a 'less than physically perfect' offspring had been overwhelming. And the years of patience needed to cope with the special needs that such a child brings also took its toll. And to dwell on the uncertain future of such a child once the parent is no longer able to be there brings immeasurable stress and feelings of hopelessness. But now, Josh had found a way that bridged his inability to articulate his love and gratitude for his loving mother. In short, Josh wanted his mother to be, if just for a moment, proud of her son.

As the crowd cheered hysterically, Josh caught then overtook the rest of the runners. As Josh's mother witnessed this, she too ran with everything she had toward the finish line losing her sunbonnet then small handbag in the mad dash. And as Josh crossed the finish line first and collapsed into the arms of the waiting official hugger; his body quickly returned to the twisted frame that it always had been. No sooner had Josh fell into the arms of the official; the young boy looked for his mother who was now at his feet hugging him and smothering him with kisses telling him how much she loved 'her little man.' Years of frustration and bottled up emotion were now streaming down the cheeks of Josh's mother. And her hold on Josh was now an embrace of wanted forgiveness that wasn't necessary because Josh's unconditional love for his mother was stronger than any guilt.

As I looked around, I could still see people looking in amazement at each other in an attempt to try and figure out what had just occurred. Others were still cheering and others were spilling onto the field trying to make their way to Josh so they could just touch him as if he were a saintly apparition sent by Jesus himself. This celebration of life went on for several minutes and all the while, Josh and his mother never broke their embrace. It was as if they had been reunited for the first time after being separated at birth.

When the hysteria finally subsided, a good Samaritan who had retrieved Josh's mother's hat and handbag handed them to her and told her how blessed she was to have such a child as did countless others. And like the others who paid their respects and compliments, she thanked them and told them each and all, 'Yes, I am blessed!' And with their arms around each other, Josh and his mother both made their way past the grandstand only to be given a standing ovation. And on their way to the exit, they stopped at my location where Josh's mother formerly introduced her son to me. And as I shook his hand, I too told him I was proud to make his acquaintance. Josh just smiled that boyish smile as if it was just another day and with no mention of his accomplishment or the gold medal he had won worn around his neck, he returned the favor by simply saying, 'This is my Mom.'

Later in the day, while at the hotel, we were packing our things for the short trip home when Bill approached me and thanked me for everything I had done regarding the event. I advised him that the pleasure was all mine and we shook hands and I started my drive home on I-95. As I drove home, I thought of Josh, his mother, and how much richer my life had become. And with this particular benchmark now in my life, the world, like the image in the eyepiece of a telescope, became a little clearer.

The Snake

I'm pretty sure that every work place has its "snake". Ours was Officer Steve Lobake. Steve was a road patrol officer for several years but went up to detective division to help out for a short while. Please don't get me wrong. Steve was a great cop in every sense of the word and one funny guy. But he was a snake even more so and eventually picked up the nickname of *The Snake* and justifiably.

Nothing was beyond the realm of *the Snake*. And that applied to his private life as well as his on duty antics. Unfortunately, my locker was located right next to *the Snake's* locker in the officer's locker room and he eventually obtained my lock combination from watching me day after day opening my locker. The guy was patient if nothing else. One day, *the Snake* got into my locker and took a small quantity of my police business cards that had my name and I.D. number on them. And he only took a few so I wouldn't miss them.

That night, *the Snake* hit several local bars and night clubs and approached as many women as he could and made sure he was as much of an insulting ass as he could be while trying to pick up anyone and everyone with a skirt.

As he did this, he handed out my business cards before parting company and told the unfortunate women to look him up when they felt lucky. Unfortunately (for me), *The Snake* and I looked somewhat alike. We both had brown hair, a mustache and about the same age and build. The following day, several of these women came into the station with my business card in hand to file a complaint on Officer Smith for being rude, obnoxious and unprofessional. The brass entertained all complaints regardless of their nature or validity and was happy to speak to her.

When I arrived at work, I was called up stairs. Nothing good ever happens "upstairs" and I was advised that I was in hot water for my behavior off duty. When I was told what the behavior was I, as usual, denied any involvement. When I was shown one of my business cards that one of the women had left behind and told that all the women had described a white male fitting my description, it began to come together. I knew *the Snake* was somehow behind it and it would do no good to try and place the blame on him. He was too smart for that and would have an alibi ready. Instead, I was lucky enough to prove my whereabouts the previous night and had witnesses to support it. I would deal with *the Snake* my own way!

A few days passed and I hadn't said anything to anyone about being one upped by *the Snake*. Then one evening, several units including myself received a call about a carload of drunks skipping out on their tab at a local bar. I located the vehicle a short time later and stopped it with the assistance of a couple of other units. The officer who was assigned to the bill-skip incident arrived and asked the occupants of the vehicle to exit the vehicle while he spoke to the driver. While he did this, I kept an eye on this big stupid good ole boy that was obviously intoxicated and agitated with the cops for stopping them. I could tell the drunk just wanted a reason to fight. As he leaned against the trunk of the vehicle, he tried to put a cigarette in his mouth and light it. I politely asked him not to smoke for our safety and his until we parted company. It was just a routine request. But it made no difference to him and he lit the cigarette anyway. I calmly removed the cigarette from between his lips and again requested politely that he not smoke. I turned my head for a few seconds away from the drunk to check on the other officers and upon turning around found him with a lit cigarette again between his lips. Again, I removed the cigarette and removed the pack from in his pocket along with his matches and repeated the request one last time. The drunk then demanded his cigarettes back because it was his *right* to smoke any time he wanted to.

I'm not sure what constitutional amendment that fell under but I assured him it wasn't going to happen. That was enough for him and the fight was on. The fight was short lived and once in custody, he was taken to the station to be booked. As I filled out the paperwork, the drunk yelled and demanded that his smoking rights be observed and he just threw a general fit until he finally ran out of steam about an hour later.

Pranks were common among the officers back then and it was not out of the ordinary to have a supply of prank equipment/supplies in our briefcases or nearby when opportunity knocked. In my case, I specialized in itching-powder and cigarette-loads and I now smelled an opportunity for a little payback with *the Snake*! Among the property of the prisoner was his pack of cigarettes and that book of matches. I promptly took all but one smoke from the pack and all but one match from the matchbook and laid both in plain view on the booking counter; but not before packing my last four cigarette-loads in the end of the drunk's one remaining cigarette. I wanted to make sure he got the right cigarette and had a nice flame to set it off. In those days, one could smoke in public buildings and ashtrays were provided and conveniently located about the station. Now, all I needed was *the Snake*!

I phoned up to the front desk and asked if the booking officer *(The Snake)* could come to my location and witness some signatures so the drunk could be released with his court date. I then released the prisoner from his cell and asked him to step up to the counter to sign his paperwork and he immediately spotted the cigarette pack I had placed near the ashtray and asked who they belong to? I made it very clear that I had no idea who they belong to. He then asked if he could have the last cigarette in the pack while he waited to be released? I agreed, and like clockwork, *the Snake* rounded the corner and came into the booking room as I had requested. I handed *the Snake* the prisoner's paperwork and told *the Snake* I would only be a moment as I left from view. As I spoke to the *Snake,* I could see the big drunk place the cigarette between his lips and tear the match from its cover to strike it. As I rounded the corner, my last recollection of that moment was *the Snake* standing next to the drunk looking over the paperwork I had just completed and the prisoner smiling as he placed the loaded cigarette between his lips that had gotten him arrested in the first place.

There was a few seconds of eerie silence before all four loads blew at once. I was expecting a good bang but this sounded more like a tire blowout on a vehicle! Then there was another few seconds of silence followed by what sounded like a truck driving through a sheet metal building.

I knew brawl was on and I was only a few feet away from the fracas but I took a few extra seconds to recall the *Snake's* business card prank and savored the moment. When I thought the *Snake* had had enough, I bolted around the corner to his assistance. As I stepped into the room, I could see both the good old boy and *the Snake* on the floor locked together like two alley cats. *The Snake* had his arms around the drunk preventing him from throwing any more punches but was unable to do anything further. I thought it best to just grab a foot from each participant and just drag both into the open cell and stand by the cell door until *the Snake* could release his grip and make a run for it.

The brawl only lasted for a moment but *the Snake's* uniform was pretty well shredded up and his hair, like an alley cat, was standing on end. He was none the worse for wear and after I brushed him off, I asked him, "What in the hell did you do to provoke my prisoner?"

The Snake took a second to get his breath and replied, "I swear, I was just standing there looking at the paperwork and I heard a loud noise and turned just in time to see this idiot pick up a wastebasket and hit me over the head with it." *The Snake* then headed for the locker room to clean himself up. At the time I didn't smoke, but I lit a cigarette anyway, sat back and replayed the event in my head over and over. This was payback at its finest!

The Snake was *the Snake* but in spite of being a relatively small sized individual, he was fearless. And when the crap hit the fan, you could count on him to the end. For a brief while, *the Snake* was assigned to the detective division to follow up on cases. This meant that he would have to go out into the community and interview people on the street in plain clothes. The street was no place to be if you happen to be white and especially a cop. And frequently, interviews turned into brawls and brawls into arrests, so a uniform officer standing by was a common practice. *The Snake* seldom missed an opportunity for a little fun.

During my rookie period, I was called upon a couple of times by *the Snake* to stand by while he interviewed someone. It was common practice then for a detective to conduct interviews with a nightstick tucked under their arm while they wrote down information in the event the encounter went sour. *The Snake* took it to the next level and made sure he was going to inflict some serious damage in the event of trouble, and actually carried a wooden table leg about three feet in length tucked under his arm that he had scavenged from an old dinette set. It was nearly as long as he was tall and it did in fact look very formidable to anyone considering making trouble.

On one particular occasion while on a street corner, I stood just a few feet behind the person being questioned while the *Snake* was interviewing (as trained) and the *Snake* jotted his notes down. The person being interviewed obviously didn't like whites or cops and he liked the *Snake* less and less as the interview progressed (obviously a good judge of character). The *Snake* was a master at insulting citizens and knew how to push just the right buttons and send these people over the edge and into a rage on demand. His ultimate goal was to have a rookie officer back him up and at just the right moment, give the 'word' to take the individual into custody and make the arrest. The 'word' or signal was the verbal command "10-15" which meant arrest/prisoner. And we were taught early on that once the signal was given, there was absolutely no hesitation or discussion about the matter and the person was cuffed and stuffed in a patrol car in a blink of an eye. This prevented any escape attempt or effort to incite a riot in most cases.

When *the Snake* thought the moment was right and the person he was interviewing was primed to fight, *the Snake* would turn to the rookie and simply say, "10-15" and the officer would instantly be involved in a brawl. You could see it coming a mile away but you couldn't do anything about it. It was no different than hearing the bell rung at a prizefight.

And when *the Snake* thought the rookie had enough "street training", he would jump in and assist in the arrest. This practice was very hard on uniforms and usually resulted in several battle scars. After work and over a beer, *the Snake* would critique the rookie's "arrest skills" and have a good laugh with the rest of the shift. How can you like someone as much as we liked the *Snake* but couldn't be happier when you saw him get his ass kicked? Strange, isn't it?

Squiggy

As long as I live, I'll never forget the first time I met Lenny Rosen. It was one day while running some errands at the sheriff's office headquarters. As I was leaving the building, this squatty middle-aged, penguin looking, pasty complexioned guy with thick black-rimmed glasses that were broken and naturally had been repaired with white first aid tape bumped into me at the door. I was in uniform at the time so he assumed I was on duty and I was available for any need that he may have. It wasn't my assigned area, but I was always willing to help anyone when I could. He was a little out of breath from having to walk from his personal vehicle, which was parked at least twenty feet away. After pushing his glasses back up the bridge of his nose, he inquired if I had one of those metal things that open locked vehicles. I said, "You mean a Slim-Jim?" "Yea, that's the thing" he said. Unfortunately I didn't and I asked why he needed one. Turns out he had parked his car against a yellow curbed no parking zone right out in front of the sheriff's office to run inside to get an application for employment and had locked his self out. I mean come on, that should have been my first clue!

Anyway, I felt sorry for him and located someone who did have an unlocking device so he wouldn't get ticketed and he thanked me. But not before asking if our agency was doing any hiring. I advised that I had little to no information about any hiring that the agency may be doing, but gave him the name of the lieutenant who was in charge of such matters and the lieutenant's phone number. I then excused myself and went about my errands. In retrospect, I realized that giving Lenny the lieutenant's name and his phone number was liken to when a professional baseball pitcher releases a pitch toward an awaiting batter and instantly knows the ball he just served up will soon be bouncing around in the parking lot just beyond the centerfield fence. In short, Lenny was a train wreck looking for a place to happen and I had just given him a location to do it in.

Sure enough, a few days later, I again ran into Lenny as he exited my district's headquarters. Upon seeing me, he stopped and thanked me again for the information and advised that the department had in fact been looking to fill a couple of openings and he was being considered. I should have just walked to the nearest intersection and laid down right then and there. Soon after, the lieutenant in charge of screening the new applicants stopped me in the hallway and in passing asked how long I had known Lenny Rosen. I explained the circumstances of our meeting and advised that I knew nothing of the peculiar little guy other than he pays little attention to no parking signs.

As fortune has it, Lenny was law enforcement certified in the state of Florida from some other agency and we were desperate for manpower at that particular point in time, so Lenny got the call. His first year of probation was spent mostly in training and keeping a low profile. But the instant Lenny came off probation and he felt comfortable, he blossomed and morphed into his true self. During his first year, Lenny managed to acquire the nickname of *Squiggy* from that greasy little TV character that played on the old *Lavern and Shirley* sitcom. The nickname *Squiggy* stuck to him so well, even the citizens called him Officer *Squiggy* on the streets. Over the next few years, it was one *Squiggy* incident and complaint after another. It got to the point where citizens coming to the station to file a complaint on Squiggy practically had to take a number and wait in line.

One hot afternoon, *Squiggy* parked his patrol vehicle in a small strip mall and decided to make his rounds on foot and conduct what he called "business checks". As he walked the sidewalk he would stick his head inside the doors of the businesses and ask the employees if everything was okay? This was a way to take himself out of service for normal calls in his zone that others would now have to handle. All the business owners and employees knew Lenny by now and dared not say anything but "Everything's just fine Officer Rosen, thanks for dropping by." The last thing a business owner wanted was *Squiggy* spending any time in their business making a pest of himself running off customers. On one occasion during one of these business checks, *Squiggy* needed to use the restroom (really bad) and asked the owner of a small three-chaired Mom and Pop barbershop if he could use their restroom? The owner, who was happy to oblige thought Lenny had to just urinate and told him to help himself. The barbershop was a one-room business that wasn't more than a couple hundred square feet in size that had a small restroom adjacent to the work/waiting area and the door to the restroom wasn't more than a step or two from the barber chairs that were always occupied with customers. Getting the green light, Lenny made haste to the bathroom closing the door behind him but not before grabbing a few magazines first. Several minutes went by and customers came and went and the two barbers on duty somehow forgot about Lenny. This was just fine with Lenny so Lenny took his time and made a thorough job of it. According to one of the barbers on duty that day, Lenny exited the restroom leaving the door wide open and without breaking stride briskly walked to the front door and exited the business without saying a word along the way.

The business owner went on to say that when Lenny opened the front door to leave, it created somewhat of a vacuum that sucked all the air that was in the bathroom out and into the occupied working area instantly. Then, as if cued, everyone, including those draped with barber cloths around their necks and in the middle of their haircuts covered their faces with their hands and ran for the front door and into the parking area for a breath of fresh breathable air as if they had just been tear-gassed.

Similar incidents occurred on two other occasions in private homes of citizens who had been burglarized and had summoned the police for a report. Again, Lenny would ask to use the restroom and would be M.I.A. (missing in action) for quite some time. After exiting the restroom the homes would be uninhabitable for hours. Lenny was the only officer I had ever known who was written up for "offending the general public".

The name Lenny Rosen was known statewide. No matter where he went or whom he met, he left an impression that wasn't soon forgotten. Lenny was involved in so many controversies and complaints; citizens from the community would sometimes call for assistance but added that, "if it's Officer Squiggy you're sending just never mind". Lenny's law enforcement days ended one spring afternoon when he finally snapped altogether and the Captain had to take his badge, gun, and keys until he got mentally evaluated. Unfortunately, Lenny had made a separate set of keys and somehow managed to make his way into the fenced in police parking lot where he stole a marked patrol vehicle and went for a county wide joy ride. During the joy ride all over the county, Lenny could be heard over the radio pleading his case that it (his being suspended) was the fault of several staff officers that just had it in for him. The local media was also aware of the incident and had dispatched numerous news teams and a news helicopter in an attempt to locate him. For about an hour or so, Lenny evaded everyone looking for him and he had his own little captive audience and portable radio station.

Finally, after Lenny was located by another agency and tracked by the S.W.A.T. team for about an hour, Lenny had sense enough to realize that things were about to get ugly. Knowing that if he was captured and committed to a mental health facility, he would have no say in when he would eventually get released. But if he checked himself into a facility, he could walk out when he so desired. So Lenny drove himself to the local mental health facility where he bolted from the stolen patrol vehicle and ran to the front door where he immediately checked himself in for observation. Lenny was certifiably nuts, but not stupid!

A Horse with No Name

One of my favorite stories is of my first law enforcement boss. The agency that I worked for was a medium size agency in a very high crime area of South Florida along the Florida Gold Coast. It was a predominantly black populated area and the local government was up to its neck in shady politics and graft from decades of the Good Old Boy System and Civil Rights Carpetbaggers.

The head of the agency was a locally born and bred black activist named Chief Darmon. He was a very popular person and a leader in the black community. Just about everyone liked him regardless of his or her race or political affiliations. He related well to everyone and tried to please as many as he could despite his pitfalls. The guy just got things done! Chief Darmon did however have his problems with staying within the boundaries of law himself and eventually got wrapped up with organized crime and did some federal time under the R.I.C.O. Act.

I was told this story by several old timers who worked with Chief Darmon in his early years and to this day they swear the story is true. It goes something like this:

As a young man, Chief Darmon always wanted to be in law enforcement. From what I was told, he did well in school and resided in the rapidly growing West Palm Beach area of Palm Beach County nearly all his life. The West Palm Beach area was having its problems with racial issues and crime just like a lot of other metropolitan areas in the nineteen forties and fifties. And like other departments, they too were trying to diversify and hire as many qualified blacks and other minorities as they could in order to serve the community as best they could. Darmon was one such officer.

As a young patrol officer during the forties and fifties, the common metropolitan beat cop usually rode two per patrol vehicle. These vehicles had no radios and little to nothing else in them other than essential equipment. The only means of communication between the road officer and headquarters was a frequent stop at a "call box" that took place about every fifteen minutes or so. A "call box" was a small metal box that was mounted on numerous telephone poles on nearly every block of the city. These boxes contained a telephone that had a direct line to headquarters and/or the desk sergeant on duty. The patrolling units obtained their calls by this method and if a unit wasn't heard from for a while, other police units were sent to their area to find them and check on their safety. Another means to summon patrolling units was a flashing blue light affixed atop the tallest building in town. If patrolling units saw the blue light flashing (especially at night), they knew to stop at the nearest "call box" and call in. Also, West Palm Beach was not the developed city we know today. The bulk of the city and its population stretched only about a mile inland from the coast. From there, it was mostly wilderness and agricultural areas.

Story has it that Darmon and his partner were on patrol late one evening and received an assignment to go to the intersection of Narcissi St. and Chrysanthemum St. for some sort of disturbance. The streets in this section of the city were all named after flowers and both Darmon and his partner knew the area well, which was a good thing because all the street signs in this area had long been torn down or stolen by the local youth. Once Darmon and his partner arrived at the intersection, they were amazed to see a dead horse lying in the middle of the intersection. The horse had apparently gotten loose from a nearby farm and had found its way to the intersection where someone had apparently struck and killed it with their vehicle.

During those early years, officers on patrol had to document every call on a three by five inch index card that eventually got handed into the sergeant at the end of the officer's shift. Information on the card consisted of the location, nature of the call and a brief narrative of what the officer's actions were.

That being the case and it was Darmon's turn to write the required report, Darmon broke out the three by five inch index card for his report. But Darmon could not come even close to correctly spelling Narcissi or Chrysanthemum and neither could his partner. With no street signs to aid the spelling, Darmon improvised and did what Darmon did best. Darmon opened the trunk of the patrol vehicle and removed a length of rope. He then tied one end to the back bumper of the patrol vehicle and the other around the horse's neck and proceeded to drag the dead horse several blocks to the intersection of 1st and Oak St so he could now complete his report for his supervisor. You have to hand to him, the guy always found a way to get things done.

Close Calls

The reality of law enforcement is that at any given moment, one can get their ticket to heaven punched in a variety of ways. Even when you do everything right, things can still go terribly wrong.

There are several types of calls where law enforcement will drive like a madman in an attempt to get to their destination as fast as they can. Some of these calls consist of:

"Shootings in progress" calls

'Officer down' calls

Calls involving hurt or endangered children

And disturbances or fights at strip clubs/bar

If a call is put out over the air that there is trouble at a local strip club/bar, you can count on every patrol car within ten miles arriving within a minute or two. And I was no different.

One evening, we received such a call at a local strip club. Shortly after arrival, the officers had several intoxicated patrons out of the bar and in the parking lot sorting out the problem. The establishment advised they were too intoxicated and were annoying the girls and just wanted them out of the business for the evening and wasn't interested in pursuing any charges.

But before they could be released, names and identifications had to be checked for warrants to insure no "bad guys" slipped through our fingers. It was explained to all who were involved that once the officers had completed checking identifications, all could leave but none were permitted back in the establishment for the evening. As I spoke to one individual, his buddy, who had already been checked and cleared of any wants or warrants, stepped between myself and the person I was checking out and stated in an agitated tone: "If you take my buddy, you're going to have to take me too!" and bowed his chest towards me in an offensive posture. I politely (but firmly) advised, "Please stand aside, sir. Do not interfere. As soon as I am done, you all can be on your way and no one will be going to jail." I then escorted the man to a vehicle a few feet away and instructed him to remain there. I then returned to my original patron to finish my questioning only to be interrupted again by the same drunk insisting that if anyone went to jail, it would be him. I repeated my efforts for a second time with the drunk and added that if he interfered again with my investigation, he would be placed under arrest for disorderly intoxication.

I hadn't turned away for more than a second when he again insisted loudly that he be placed under arrest instead of his companions. That's ok with me. In an instant, he was handcuffed, patted down, and placed in the back seat of my patrol vehicle. Prior to placing anyone in your patrol vehicle, a good pat down is always conducted if you value your life.

Upon arrival at police headquarters, the prisoner was removed from my vehicle. However, during the trip the prisoner had managed to maneuver his hands from behind his back to the front by sliding them under his feet. This is not uncommon and was more annoying than anything else. He was then taken into the holding cell area. There, another officer and I conducted a more thorough search of the prisoner in the event something was missed earlier. When I asked the prisoner to remove and shake out his cowboy type boots, a small leather holster fell to the floor. Upon examining the leather holster, I could see the outline of what appeared to be a small two shot derringer type handgun. I was very familiar with these cheap throwaway type firearms. As I held the holster up for the prisoner to see, I asked where the gun was that belonged in it? At first, there was silence. I then advised that no matter where it was I was eventually going to find it. The prisoner then advised that it was in my patrol vehicle.

The prisoner was placed in a cell and I returned to my vehicle to look for the gun. When I found it and examined it, I paused and became cold with what could have been my last moments on Earth. The gun was in fact a two shot, .38-caliber derringer. To load the gun, a lever was tripped and the over and under barrels of the gun broke downwards exposing the loading end where the bullets were inserted. Both of the chambers had live hollow point rounds in them. What made it so chilling was the top chamber, which is first in the firing sequence. It had a .38-calbre bullet in it with a big dent in the primer cap indicating that the owner had attempted to fire the gun but something had caused a misfire. After it was all said and done, it turns out the drunk had maneuvered his hands from behind his back, took the gun from his boot, placed it against the back of the driver's seat and pulled the trigger. When the gun failed to go off, he dropped it and kicked it under my seat in an attempt to hide it. I recalled squeezing his boots at the bar but I felt nothing suspicious and wondered how this could have happen. I was always so careful. It was a cold reminder of what I did for living.

A few months later, I had responded to a call of a man discharging a shotgun in the back yard of a neighbor's home during a domestic dispute. I happen to be within a block or two when the call came out so my response time was only a few seconds. When I exited my patrol vehicle, I immediately heard two shotgun blasts from the rear of the home. I removed my shotgun from my dash mount, racked a shell in the chamber and walked toward the direction of the shots. When I rounded the corner of the house, the back yard became visible. There I could see a man with a shotgun shooting into an unoccupied parked vehicle. I later learned that it was his girlfriend's car and he was taking out his jealous rage on it. Upon seeing me, the man dropped his now empty shotgun and rushed me screaming for me to kill him. Before I could retreat or secure my shotgun, he was on top of me and we were rolling on the ground for control of my gun. My main effort was to stay away from the business end of the barrel and to cup and keep my hand over the trigger guard to prevent the man from firing the weapon. As we rolled on the ground, I knew help would soon be arriving and all I had to do was to stay in the fight and not lose control of the 12 gauge Remington 870 Shotgun that I was desperately clinging to. If I did lose control, I would have to do "what I had to do"! After what seemed to be an eternity, I finally heard the familiar voice of a fellow officer yelling, "I've got him back here, he's on the ground 10-94, 10-94" over his radio, (which was the code for emergency back-up).

Out of the corner of my eye, I could see a small group of blue uniforms break from the shadows of a nearby street light and charge around the same corner of the house I had just rounded a few seconds earlier. Headquarters had tried to raise me on the radio to see if I was okay and I was not answering and more calls were coming in from 911 that shots were being fired. That could only mean one thing and that prompted the cavalry! If there is any reason to believe an officer is down and/or in trouble, look out!

As the group of officers sprinted to within a few yards of the fight, the madman managed to finally get his finger on the trigger. The Remington 870 was a pump type shotgun and I knew I had only one shot to deal with at a time. With my last ounce of energy, I directed the muzzle of the gun upward just in time to direct the following blast skyward that stripped a nearby tree of half its leaves. The shotgun's muzzle flash momentarily lit up the responding officers like someone had just taken their photo using a flash bulb. That instant in time will be forever be imbedded in my memory. I wish that it had been a photo and had captured the expressions on their faces. As critical and intense as it was, it's kind of comical to see what you look like when you're shot at! The madman and I were peeled apart and he was taken to the E.R. to be stitched up (needless to say) and I got really, really drunk that night.

Danger can come from anywhere, any time. *The Snake* and I had arrived at a stabbing call where a woman had stabbed her husband multiple times in the back with a steak knife because he refused to give her the last cigarette in the pack of all things. On the last stab, she took the cheap steak knife as it was imbedded in her husband back and bent the handle upward so her husband couldn't reach around and grab the handle and pull out (charming woman). She was placed in cuffs and we were standing by while the medics worked on her old man as he lay on the living room floor leaking like sieve.

As the medics worked on Pop, Junior, (who was about nine years old) appeared in the living room from nowhere, saw white cops and fire personnel in the house and without saying a word, picked up the knife that was just moments before embedded in Pop's back and attempted to stab a medic. I had no sooner put Junior in a bear hug when his older sister, (about twelve) came running through the front door, also saw what was going on and disappeared into the kitchen. A couple of seconds later, she reappeared with another steak knife and charged another medic and was subdued by *the Snake* after a short flight across the living room!

Sometimes, you don't realize what you're into before it is too late and you're committed. One Saturday evening, I closed up a local club that was located in a beachfront mall on the island. When I say I closed it up, I mean I was the last one out of the door before the owner followed and locked the doors about 3 a.m. I had a pretty good buzz on and was feeling little pain. I lived just a few moments away and had walked to the bar not wanting to drive anticipating a high blood alcohol content level at the end of the evening.

The club was at the end of a corridor in a beachfront mall and overlooked several other businesses that had long closed earlier that evening. Upon exiting the door of the club, I was just in time to witness three black males throw a large cinder block through the showroom window of an all leather men's store not more than ten feet from me. The broken glass was still falling from the steel frame of the window as all three black males rushed in and grabbed arms full of leather jackets and other high priced items and ran from the business to a waiting vehicle parked just a few feet away on the street. I've heard of people sobering up in an instant when their adrenalin kicks in, but I'd never had it happen to me until then. I wore a five shot .38-caliber revolver on my ankle when I was off duty and up until then I thought it was a hassle. I quickly knelt and drew my revolver and found myself running after two of three of the males not knowing that the third had exited the store behind me. In the confusion, we were all running as a group and I was in the middle. You would think that someone would have noticed the white guy not carrying anything but they didn't.

As we reached the two door type vehicle, the stolen merchandise was tossed into the vehicle that was already half full of other stolen property and everyone scrambled to get inside. I somehow got shoved behind the steering wheel while the others crammed in the remaining door and crawled through open windows on top of each other.

In as short as time it took for us to get in the vehicle, it took even less time for everyone to exit the vehicle once they saw the unfamiliar white guy behind the wheel with a gun in his hand. It was like someone kicked over a can of cockroaches as they bolted from the car. With my free hand, I did manage to get a grasp on one of the suspects as he flew by. His momentum carried us both to the pavement where I managed to maneuver myself on top. From there, I wedged most of the 2-inch barrel of my Smith and Wesson up the nostril of my only capture. It was a little piece of heaven. Alone at 3am with a burglar in the act, with no one around and having your revolver shoved up his nose. I was only allowed to savor the moment for a few seconds when a passing car with several people slowed to get a closer look. As they slowed, I blurted out that I was a police officer and to please call 911 immediately and tell the dispatcher I needed assistance. I also asked that they tell the dispatcher that the remaining two suspects were on foot and west bound across the bridge. Within seconds, I could hear the sirens heading my way. After it was all over, I learned that this group, (who had all been captured by responding units) had been on a three-day crime spree. The car they used was stolen locally and the group had burglarized several businesses and had also robbed several victims at gunpoint. I couldn't help but smile a little when I got a commendation from the captain a few days later. It's a good thing it never went to trial. I was so drunk that night, I barely remembered leaving the club that evening or going home.

When in law-enforcement, the "bogeyman" lurks around every corner. One never knows during a career how many times fate spared your life. In the early eighties, it was estimated that one in every three vehicles stopped by law-enforcement during traffic stops contained illegal firearms. And you wondered how many times a person with a gun in their hand ready to use it was behind that door you just knocked on but got no answer? I'm still not sure how I merited a guardian angel but it was obvious to me early on that someone was watching over me!

Dr. Dolce

Officers were injured fairly regularly in lovely Tropical Beach. It was frequently enough that we had our own departmental physician/surgeon on call. His name was Dr. Joseph Dolce. He was a stocky guy, in his late sixties, silver hair, and had the demeanor of Michigan badger caught in a foot trap. He was a retired army colonel and surgeon and quite a colorful guy. Dr. Dolce's military specialty was gunshot wounds. While in his office one day for some broken ribs, I couldn't help but notice an extremely large display case that filled an entire wall of his office. In the glass case was every bullet manufactured by man in the last fifty years. It started on one end with a .22 caliber short projectile and progressed to a 20mm. It was pretty impressive. Along with the collection of bullets were artifacts from his career in the U.S. Army like medals, campaign ribbons and photos.

One photo caught my eye and stood out from the rest. It was a photo of Dr. Dolce with what appeared to be a judge, but not just any judge. It was Supreme Court Chief Justice Earl Warren of the Supreme Court of the early sixties period. It struck me very odd that the elderly doctor that was now treating my injuries was at one time was rubbing elbows with a member of the Supreme Court, and Chief Justice Earl Warren nonetheless.

When the doctor saw my interest in the photo, he said, "What do you think about that?" Naturally, I said I was impressed and asked about the circumstances leading up to the photo. It's not everyone who gets a photo opportunity with such a figure. As Dr. Dolce pulled up a stool and settled in, I knew I had taken the bait and was in for a story.

He started with telling me of his long and distinguished career as an army surgeon and how he became an expert on gunshot wounds while serving in WW-II and later Korea. Being a field surgeon during WWII and Korea provided lots of on the job training. Then he asked if I knew what the Warren Commission was. Being a little of a history buff, I advised that I did and asked the connection between him and Chief Justice Warren. In November of 1963, President Johnson created a commission to investigate President Kennedy's assassination and appointed Chief Justice Earl Warren in charge. This was known as the Warren Commission. Even to this day, there is speculation as to whether the commission's findings were credible or if it was an elaborate cover-up for some conspiracy to assassinate Kennedy.

Dr. Dolce advised that he was brought into the commission as an expert witness to review the president's autopsy findings and to make a judgment on if the wounds found on the president were consistent with the "one shooter theory", or if he thought there may have been more than one shooter. Dolce advised that he poured over countless autopsy photos, statements from attending physicians, the actual bullets recovered and the infamous 8mm film of the actual shooting and examined the crime scene. Dolce was emphatic, and I mean emphatic that no "one shooter" from a "single location" could have created the end results. And this was conveyed to the Warren Commission but was ignored. When he spoke of the commission, it wasn't in endearing terms. He knew in his mind what the government spoon-fed the public was an out and out lie. To this day, a good portion of the report still remains sealed to the public. And any information within the document made public has quite a bit of "blacked out" information edited out. To Dolce, there was only one reason for this, a cover up.

From time to time, Dr. Dolce would be called to the station where he would have to stitch up someone who got in the way of a nightstick or brick. And in most cases, the person needing treatment would not want it (a prisoner). But nonetheless, it would have to be done. In those days, the officers would have to physically hold down the person being treated while Doc Dolce threaded up a needle and commenced to stitch'in.

The more the person struggled, spit and cursed at the doctor, the more the likelihood they would arrive at county jail looking like some sort of Frankenstein fresh from the laboratory. The only thing missing would be that bolt sticking out on both sides of their neck. Sometimes the Doc would get frustrated and would simply hand the prisoner the needle and thread and tell them to do it themselves. But when it came to an officer being injured, Dr. Dolce was the best. With his battleground demeanor and calming voice, a wounded or injured officer couldn't ask for a more knowledgeable and compassionate bedside doctor. You knew you were in the hands of the best when you opened your eyes and saw Doc Dolce standing next to you, and it happened often.

Leaving It At Work

There are countless occupations where one could 'bring their work home' with them and it may or may not affect their home life in a negative manner. Law-enforcement was and still is definitely not one of them!

Alcoholism, divorce and even suicide are common among law enforcement. For those plagued with being a part of those horrible statistics, life and the inability to cope with their job and personal life are a daily struggle. As I've mentioned before, the good Lord must have assigned a guardian angel to keep one eye on me from the start. From my early years in law-enforcement, it was very apparent to me that quite a few who had spent any time in the business were displaying behavior like excessive drinking as soon as they were off duty, had domestic troubles, constantly displayed aggression, and some just had a terrible outlook on humanity in general. I learned quickly that what happens at work stays at work with no exceptions. This important rule resulted in my ability to make friends outside of law-enforcement, sleeping at night, digesting my food, and not think the sun rose and sat on the department. You're a human being first and a cop second. To this day, some of the more unpleasant experiences from my career are still a little difficult to recall in detail because I didn't "take it home with me" and let it into my private life. No matter how hard you try, some things just follow you home. You wouldn't be human being if they didn't. The number one thing that just knocked me down was the calls concerning children. Adults ask for a lot of their own misery, either directly or indirectly. And as much as you sympathize with them in most cases, they will turn right around and go right back into the same situation that got them in trouble in the first place. But the children are truly the innocent victims of abuse, neglect and circumstance. When this happens, my heart simply breaks in two and it's all I can do to just place one foot in front of the other as I walk away from the call.

On a rain slick day in the early afternoon, a call came over the radio indicating that a two-vehicle accident with injuries had just occurred on a local highway just a few blocks from my location. The radio also indicated that among the injured were children. As I listen to the radio, I heard two units arrive just seconds before me. I quickly assigned the second unit that arrived to control traffic so the situation wouldn't become worse with another accident while the other officer and I attended to the occupants of both vehicles. It appeared that a four door sedan had rear ended a large panel truck causing quite a bit of damage to the sedan but little damage to the truck. The driver of the truck was uninjured as was the female driver of the sedan because she had taken the time to buckle herself in securely. However the female smelled of alcohol and had in fact a large cup filled with ice and what appeared to be a "screwdriver" mixture still lying on the floor under the gas pedal.

Normally, this would have ended with a D.U.I. arrest and that would have been the end of it. But the female also had her two small children in the vehicle with her. A one year old was asleep on the back seat unsecured at the time of the accident and suffered internal injuries. And a two-year-old boy was standing in the front passenger seat unsecured at the moment of impact. The impact threw the standing child face first into the windshield resulting in a vicious laceration that went from temple to temple along the hairline of his forehead. The child's scalp was pealed back nearly to his neck exposing his scull. As I held the still conscious child in my arms waiting for the medics to arrive, his big brown eyes stared into mine and the only word I can come up with is *helpless*. I too had a two-year-old boy at home with those same brown eyes waiting for me to get home. Tears mixed with rage as I watched the intoxicated mother survey the damage to her car apparently uncaring of the injured child. But I was a police officer and any display of emotions had to be controlled and dumped at another location and at another time. That's just the way it is.

Summer time pretty much anywhere means hot kids wanting to cool off together from the two year old child playing. But now, it was terrifyingly quiet. Instantly, her attention went to the barrier wedged in the kitchen slider. What she saw started a chain reaction no mother should have to endure. The wooden barrier was partially dislodged and a gap of only a few inches between the barrier and the door showed. Nonetheless, it was large enough for a small child to wiggle through. The young mother crashed through the barrier and stopped short of the water filled tiled pool to see her baby lying motionless at the bottom of the shallow end.

When the first units arrived, they found her on her knees in the kitchen with the baby in her arms rocking it and sobbing uncontrollably and unresponsive. She was in shock and didn't remember calling 911 or even jumping into the swimming pool. The hardest thing I've ever had to do was to pry the baby from its mother's arms. And it is something I pray I never have to do again. As the medics loaded the lifeless infant into the ambulance, they allowed the mother to be by its side for the token ride to the emergency room as they "worked" the infant. Now someone had to call the father at his workplace and deliver the news that the child he just kissed goodbye at breakfast is dead and he needed to go to his wife at the hospital. How does one just shake a call like that off and move on to the next call? I'll tell you how. You swallow hard, take a deep breath, and think of it as your job and nothing more. Then you take the next call.

Another lovely day, a detective called from a local hospital and asked for a uniform officer to come to the emergency room in anticipation of making an arrest. A woman had brought an infant into the emergency room with severe burns over half its lower body. The mother explained that the child had accidentally dumped a pan of hot water on itself in the kitchen by reaching up on the stove and grabbing a pan. When I arrived, you could hear the child screaming before you even entered the room. The child was two or three years old at the most with long golden hair and big blue eyes. I could actually feel the horrific pain within the screams she emitted one after another. I couldn't imagine the suffering she was going through. The detective handed me a camera and asked if I would take some photos for him for evidence. Before I could enter the emergency room cubical, I had to put a gown and mask on because of the risk of infection. When I entered the cubical, I was horrified. The less than twenty-pound child had absolutely no skin from the waist down. Where skin once was, it now resembled raw steak that one might see in a supermarket display case. It was obvious that the malnourished baby had been dipped in scalding hot water for some unknown reason. It came out later that the child would not stop crying and the live-in boyfriend had dipped the little girl in a tub of hot water for punishment as the mother looked on.

The mother went to jail immediately and the boyfriend was picked up a week later. A sergeant was assigned to escort the boyfriend from the time the cuffs went on to the time he was turned over to the jail officials for fear of something happening to him in route. Once incarcerated, he was placed in isolation for fear of something happening at the hands of the prisoners. Even criminals have standards and will tolerate only so much.

Any routine call can turn into an emotional hurtle. Because of the large elderly population in South Florida, the passing of a senior citizen becomes routine after a while and not a lot of thought is given to them if assigned one. As a road sergeant, part of my duty was to drop in on certain calls just to see if the deputy was handling the call properly or if I could be of assistance.

If death was from what appeared to be natural causes and a physician would sign the death certificate, things just fell into place and for the most part; it was just matter of notifying the desired funeral home. . One such call was dispatched out during my shift involving an elderly man who had apparently passed away in his sleep only to be found by a neighbor the following day when he didn't answer the door. The officer was on scene and in the process of handling the call when I dropped by to see if everything was going okay or if he needed any assistance.

As I entered the elderly person's condominium, it looked as any would with medications and photos of the grandchildren about and artifacts strewed about the living room. The officer filled me in on the circumstances and told me the deceased was still in the bedroom awaiting the funeral home personnel. As I entered the bedroom, the outline of the person could be made out from under the sheet that was now covering the body. To this point it was just another call. But as I pulled back the sheet to see the face of the man under it, I momentarily lost my breath.

Beneath the sheet with his dull lifeless eyes still open was my good friend Iggy. Iggy had long been retired from somewhere in New York and was the ranger at the local golf course not far away. He had a take-home golf cart that you'd see him and his little Boston terrier in regularly shopping or just cruising and visiting other retired citizens. Iggy would always flag me down if I was in a patrol vehicle or make it a point to stop and talk with me. At the end of every encounter, Iggy would tell me how I was "one of the good ones" and how much he enjoyed talking to me. His smile went from ear to ear and his heavy New York accent made it obvious where he was from. On the golf course, Iggy was always glad to stop and give pointers from time to time to those who needed them. Most golf course rangers were gruff and short tempered with the customers, but not Iggy. He would stop and smile and politely ask if there was a problem or ask if there was anything he could do to assist. He had children but he seldom spoke to them for some unknown reason and his loving wife had long passed before him. Before I returned the sheet to the position I found it, I closed Iggy's eyes and said my goodbyes. Iggy's little dog was given to the friend and I then personally made the call to the son in New York informing him of his father's death. The first thing the son asked was the location of his father's gold wedding band. There was no inquiry as to the manner of death or if his father suffered. It was now crystal clear why Iggy and his son didn't talk more than they did. It was a hell of a way to say goodbye to a friend.

Rewards

If I had to choose just one call of my three decades of law enforcement career to keep and take with me when I pass, it would be the following encounter.

As awful as death related calls are, there are some that can be quite rewarding and or endearing in a spiritual kind of way. On an abnormally cool fall morning, a routine senior citizen natural death call was dispatched out and as the road sergeant, I too responded. I entered the condominium apartment and spoke to the officer assigned. After being briefed, the officer told me the wife was in the bedroom with the deceased and taking it pretty hard.

When I entered the bedroom of the elderly couple, I could see the deceased who had passed in his sleep, covered with a sheet still lying on his side of the bed. Beside him was his wife of over fifty years sitting on an old antique rocking chair. As I watched her, I couldn't help but wonder how many times over the decades of their marriage one of them sat in that chair watching over the other during a sickness or injury? The old woman had her husband's arm exposed and his ring hand was cupped in hers on her lap as if she was trying to comfort him one last time. The old woman looked like she had stepped out of a Norman Rockwell painting. Her face plainly showed the years and her frail frame barely held her upright. The front of her terrycloth house robe was soaked and stained from a steady torrent of tears over the last couple of hours. But now because she had wept so much, she was void of any more tears and couldn't produce more if she tried. She was empty of tears like she was empty of life itself. Her partner in life, her reason for living, the reason she opened her eyes each morning had gone on without her. In her mind, she was now alone and helpless with nothing but faded memories of the love of her life. I quietly pulled up a chair and sat beside her. It was several moments before I spoke. It took that long just to think of something comforting to say. I knew that whatever I said couldn't ease the pain and fear. For the first time in her life, she was alone and I was somehow feeling the loneliness with her.

I knew that the funeral home would be arriving soon and the sight of seeing her lifelong companion being placed on a cold gurney and wheeled from the warmth of their home would be agonizing to say the least. The time had come for her to release her husband's hand for the last time. I gently took her hand and separated hers from her husband's and replaced his hand with mine. When I did, our eyes met and it was like she knew that their lives together were finally over. We both stood and walked into the kitchen where I poured her a glass of water and we sat at the kitchen table. I was careful to seat her with her back to the hall so she couldn't see the removal of the body.

As we sat and talked, the other officer on scene had managed to make contact with a daughter who lived an hour or so away. The daughter advised that she would be in route along with her husband to tend to the old woman. With the efficiency of a wrecker service, the funeral home personnel arrived, loaded the body and quickly left along with the other officer leaving the old woman and me alone. As we sat, she regressed back to the days when she and her deceased husband first met and told me of their life together. She spoke of their struggles, their accomplishments and of their love for each other through thick and thin.

At first, my heart broke in two listening to her life story, but after a few more moments, I realized that she was reaching inward and drawing on the strength she had beneath her frail frame. An hour or so passed like it was only a few moments and finally her daughter walked through the front door and embraced the old woman. Enough time had passed now that the old woman was able to cry once again along with her family. Without saying anything, I left my business card on the table with a hand written note on the back for the family to contact me if there was anything else I could assist them with and I slipped out unnoticed.

Three or four days later while at headquarters, dispatch called and advised me that I had guests in the lobby who wished to see me. Usually the "guests" were unhappy citizens who want to complain on an officer or people who were upset over a ticket. Sometimes, it was friends or family of someone who has been arrested and they need information on their current location or the location of property or the vehicle they were in at the time they were arrested. As I entered the lobby area, I observed five or six well dressed people and a short elderly woman dressed all in black that I quickly recognized as the woman who lost her husband a few days prior. Before I could say anything, the little woman turned and shuffled toward me and stopped at my feet. She then lifted the black vial from her face, cupped my face in her wrinkled little hands and kissed my check. As our eyes met once again she simply said, "Thank you young man," and she turned to her daughter, and with her assistance they all walked out of the building without saying another word to an awaiting car. To me, that was the embodiment of what an officer is. Every bad guy you put away will always get out and will more than likely repeat their crimes. The memory of the old woman thanking me for just being there will always remain with me as long as I live.

All too often, the thought of having to use deadly force comes up as a topic and rightfully so. Can we, if the moment presents itself, take a life? It was always in the back of our minds. Another issue that comes up from time to time that isn't discussed all that much is the exact opposite of the question before: Can we bring a life into the world if called upon?

I've considered myself an outdoorsman most of my life. Cleaning critters of all shapes and sizes and being around a fair amount of birthing activity on the farm exposed me to quite a bit of carnage. I've also had some paramedic training along with the standard first aid training that most officers receive. So one would think that a little thing like delivering a baby wouldn't be a real big thing… Guess again! Like most medical calls, police are usually sent along with the ambulance in the event they are needed. It is the old, 'better to have them there and not need them instead of not sending them along and needing them'. So every medical and fire call that is sent out is now routinely accompanied by a police unit until it is determined that they are not needed.

Late one evening, I received a call from dispatch that a 911 medical call had been transferred to the fire department in regards to a pregnant woman in labor. When the address was given, I happen to be practically right in front of the house and I advised dispatch that I was there. Dispatch then advised that the medics were just clearing another call and would be coming from the local hospital about fifteen minutes away. Before I could knock on the front door, an excited father-to-be opened the door and ushered me into the living room. There, his very pregnant wife was laying on her back on the sofa with one leg draped over the back and the other on the floor. The man explained he too was an officer and that this was his first child. They had already contacted the doctor by phone and the doctor told the father that the pains were false labor and not to be overly concerned. It was about this moment in time the wife let out with a scream reminiscent to that of Janet Leigh in the shower scene in Psycho that made the hair on my arms stand up like asparagus shoots. I looked at the husband and exclaimed, 'That's a false labor scream?' As the husband got the doctor on the phone again, I attended to the mother-to-be who was now clawing the furniture like a bobcat shredding rabbit. As much as I didn't want to, it was time for a "peek". Mom was wearing only a sheet and a pair of fuzzy house slippers so obtaining a peek was only a matter of lifting and looking. After excusing myself and doing so, I immediately got on my radio and asked dispatch the current location of the damn ambulance? After being advised that the ambulance was at least another ten minutes out, I told the father-to-be to advised the doctor on the other end of the line that Mom was crowning and things were about to get interesting in the living room.

When delivering a baby, there are only a few things to remember to keep the event from getting out of hand. And so far, nature was in charge and doing well without a lot of assistance from me. I was busy and didn't see the flashing lights of the arriving ambulance or hear the sirens as the fire department and medics pulled up in front of the home. As the medics scurried into the room, they were just in time to take the handoff (the child) from me and attend to the woman. After tidying up a bit, the happy new father and

I comforted the new mother who was doing well and was anxious to see her new daughter. That was some shift!

For the next twelve or thirteen years, that officer/ new dad (who was from another jurisdiction) and his daughter would make it a point to drop by the station or stop me while on patrol to say hello and we would talk of the little girl's progress at school or things going on in her life. It was nice that they made me a part of her life and allowed me to watch her grow. I really enjoyed that and wonder where she is now.

O.P.E.C.

When I was on patrol, I made it a habit to look into every crack and crevasse large enough to crawl into in my assigned zone. You never knew when you might be called upon to chase some idiot into one of the cracks or crevasse and I didn't like surprises. So I spent a lot of time out of my vehicle and on foot just walking and looking.

One day while patrolling the island, I came upon an over-grown driveway to (what appeared to be) nowhere that disappeared into the undergrowth. It was just off the main road by the ocean and headed in the direction of the beach that was only a hundred yards or so away. At first, I thought it was just where some off road vehicles had worn down the vegetation getting to the beach. Nonetheless, it was time to get out of the patrol vehicle and explore. After a few moments of walking and kicking brush to one side, a large white two-story home came into view. It was obvious that the previous inhabitants had been gone for months as the paint was pealing from neglect and one or two windows were broken from the untrimmed tree limbs that were slowly engulfing the structure.

As I approached the house, I could see cobwebs, hornet nests, and debris covering everything. The driveway led to a garage under the structure. In the garage was a washer and dryer that still looked usable and a couple of storage rooms. A staircase from the garage lead upwards to another stairs that ended at the main entrance located on the side of the home. The main door leading inside was slightly ajar and was easily opened exposing a very large room with cathedral ceilings, hardwood floors and walls and an eastern exposure made entirely of one wall that was all sliding glass doors. In it's time, it had too have been simply beautiful. From the living room, one had a magnificent view of the Atlantic Ocean and beach. The all hardwood living room was the size of a half court basketball court with the ocean only about one hundred feet away. Wow! The rest of the house was a little rough, but nothing a little soap and water wouldn't fix. As I surveyed the rest of the house, I could see signs that young people were using it as a hang out and I wondered who owned it? Greg, (my roommate) and I were looking for a place a little closer to work and I thought what a great place this would make. However if this were a rental home, it would be way out of our price bracket I thought. But with a little logic and reasoning, who knows?

On my way out of the jungle like property, I managed to locate a realty sign and copied down the phone number and the person's name that was on it. Without delay, I called the number and spoke to a woman on the other end that advised she was realtor who had that particular listing. She advised that the property was listed for seven million dollars but it was currently tied up in probate court and would probably remain so for at least another year or two. She then asked the nature of my call. In a professional manner, I advised that while on patrol, I came across the house and property and had had the occasion on more than one instance to run young people out of the house who were drinking and/or vandalizing the property. I advised her that if a minor injures him/herself while on the property or in the house, someone may be civilly liable and it would be smart to get someone to at least stay there until the house is disposed of. It would just be a matter of turning the water and electric on and cleaning the place up a bit. "Well I have no idea who I could get to stay there. Do you?" she said. If smiling made noise, you could have heard mine on the other end of the phone! "Well I don't know," I said. "The place is kind of a wreck and would take a lot of repair. My roommate who is an officer also and I are currently looking for a place closer to work. What kind of offer would you make for us to move in and tend to it until it's disposed of?" I asked. "How about rent free?" she said. "Just pay for your utilities and it is yours until it's bull dozed?" she said. Wasting no time, I said, "You have got yourself a deal. Fax me the agreement, and the room-mate and I will sign it and have it back to you a.s.a.p." I agreed.

As soon as I got off the phone, I radioed Greg who was also working and asked him to meet me at the end of the driveway of our new home. When he arrived, we did a walkthrough of our new beach house and we giggled like two June brides at the check-in desk of a motel. By the end of the shift, word was out that somehow Smitty and Greg had scored big time and party central had arrived. It was our finest moment!

With the help of some of the crew, the place was soon cleaned, debris hauled away and Greg and I had our party palace for the rich and famous. Naturally, when speaking of Smitty and Greg's party beach house in the presence of the wife, girlfriends, or some supervisors, one had to use a code name. One just couldn't say they were going to Smitty and Greg's over on the island. They would instantly be tracked down and hauled away. I think it was Dave, the K-9 guy, who came up with the *O.P.E.C.* name because of the lavishness and value of the home and property. So from that day forward, if we spoke of our place, we referred to it as O.P.E.C. (Organization of the Petroleum Exporting Countries) !

In no time at all fellow officers started to pour in and become regulars. O.P.E.C. was isolated which made it a good place to hide out when one was working and the liquor store was just a short hop away, which made it the unofficial police union hall at times. Many decisions concerning labor contracts were discussed at O.P.E.C. as was getting caught up on all the latest gossip and sports. The doors were never locked because someone with a badge was generally there 24/7. Either someone needed a place to bring a female companion, hide out from the spouse or we were hosting a kegger or luau on the beach. In any case, swim suit clad bodies of the conscious and unconscious variety were a common sight day and night. Of the entire island, there were only two actual homes left standing that could lay claim to their own personal beach and we were one of them. Hotels and condominiums had swallowed up the rest of the island's beautiful beachfront. O.P.E.C. was so popular, one afternoon I was sitting on a bench in the hall of the county courthouse preparing to testify in a trial when I overheard two uniform officers from another jurisdiction talking about a house on the beach on the island. Well, there were only two houses that I knew of, so it caught my attention.

According to one of the two officers, there were two other officers living at the house that were suppose to be involved in some serious drug smuggling and were living the high life from their illegal profits. I leaned over and politely interrupted and advised that I couldn't help but hear their conversation and asked exactly what kind of drugs and how much were they talking about?

One officer told me that he had heard that cigarette boats, (a fast off shore speed boat) had been seen several times beaching themselves in front of the house and bails of pot were seen unloaded and taken into the house. The officer went on to say that the house and the officers living there were under constant surveillance and arrests were expected soon. I then told both of the officers not to believe everything they hear and that I was sure there was nothing to the gossip and rumors. One officer then spoke up and asked how I could be so sure. I smiled and replied that I was one of the drug smuggling officers that lived there, and the only thing I've carried from the beach to the house was sand in my shorts! I laughed and got up and walked away. Just a footnote on that however; apparently an overzealous detective from our own department was seen on more than one occasion in the woods trying to conceal himself behind a palm tree while watching O.P.E.C. in an attempt to *get the goods* on someone doing something illegal. I guess he was part of the same gossiping click or possibly the origin of the rumors that the two clucking hens I spoke to at the courthouse belonged to.

Sometimes when we knew this detective was watching, some of the guys would have some fun and act suspicious just to fire him up. Once, a couple of fellow officers called and said that they would be over in a few minutes to watch a football game and would be bringing a couple of six packs. I had seen this idiot detective earlier while washing laundry in the basement creeping around in the woods so I tipped the guys off who were coming over that they would be watched when they got here by "our friend". Before long, I saw their car come up the driveway and stop behind the house and both officers exited the vehicle and paused for a few seconds. They then scanned the area carefully and then pulled their guns and walk to the trunk. While one played *look out*, the other opened the trunk and remove the brown paper bags (of beer) and secure it under his arm as if it were dope or something while the remaining officer escorted him covering his back to the door constantly on the watch. Once inside, we all gather around the bedroom window overlooking the woods and watched the delighted detective run from sight to document his observations.

Cops have little use for other cops that delighted in "getting the goods" on their coworkers. Don't get me wrong; bad law-enforcement needs to be weeded out at all cost! But this was one of those guys that chose to rise through the ranks by cutting the legs out from under other officers rather than by advancing on his own merits. And I'm sure that whomever he was trying to report our activities to knew how much of a loon he was anyway because no one ever questioned our characters or lifestyle. Hell, everyone from the rank of sergeant on down was a regular at O.P.E.C.!

Even when Greg and I took a break and stayed at home alone and tried to stay out of trouble, we seldom succeeded. As I mentioned prior, there were only two homes that were located right on the beachfront. Our home was one of them and the other was the house next door that belonged to a guy named John. John was a successful single stockbroker that fancied himself as the Hugh Hefner type. He was also an accommodating kind of guy so Greg and I established a working relationship with John soon after we moved into *O.P.E.C.* Because of the loud goings on and the fact that he had a somewhat of a "normal" job and needed sleep, we would give him at least a couple days notice of any parties scheduled at *O.P.E.C..* He in turn would book a room at the local Holiday Inn so not to be kept up all night. And because the two houses were separated by only about ten feet, he even presented us with a gift of a hydraulic door closer to replace the spring loaded screen door closer we had so it wouldn't sound like a gunshot being fired several times a night from people coming and going.

As I mentioned, only a few feet separated John's home and *O.P.E.C.* And for some unknown reason, both homes had very large picture windows facing each other allowing a clear view into each other's living room. Greg and I could care less, but John soon learned that having neighbors the likes of Greg and I virtually in your living room with you might create a problem when entertaining guests.

Late one evening Greg and I had both retired for the night when I heard John's restored classic Aston Martin car pull up in his driveway next door. Shortly after, I heard the sound of not one, but two car doors closing indicating that John had apparently brought home company from his evening of prowling the Palm Beach circuit. As I rolled over in bed and peeked out my bedroom window, I saw John escorting his company to his back door. I could see from John's porch light that she was a tall, young, blonde, a little tipsy and definitely a "looker"! John was about to go into a full court press and move in for the kill. Greg and I both knew the routine well by now. By the time I awoke Greg and told him what was going on; John was in full "phase one" (the spider to the fly) mode and had already fired up some classical music, had a chilled bottle of Dom Perignon Champagne in hand and was sprinting to the sofa where the stunning blond had now made herself comfortable. Unfortunately, John's sofa was directly in front of and facing his living room window that was no more than a few feet away from ours. In short, it was show time!

When there were no lights on at O.P.E.C., it was totally dark, and I mean pitch black! From John's living room looking out with no light, one would never have known there was even a house next door just a few feet away. Greg and I opened a cold beer, grabbed a bag of chips, pushed our ratty sofa up close to our living room window, put our feet up on the windowsill and settled in for the main event. The minor league Hugh Hefner didn't disappoint us.

Within just a few minutes, the two were lathered up and half dressed wallowing around on the sofa like two Roman Greco wrestlers. Greg and I had seen this movie several times before and knew this was where John normally retired to the bedroom only to reappear in his white terrycloth robe that had his initials embroidered in gold on the front and puffing on the traditional Hugh Hefner evening smoking pipe. Closing the deal was only a formality and seconds away.

While John was out of the room and changing into his battle gear, the gorgeous young blonde began to shed her remaining garments and was soon down to her bra and laced robin's egg blue panties (they were quite lovely I might add). By now, Greg and I were cheering and doing the "wave" like two idiots sitting on the fifty-yard line at a Dolphin's game. All that was missing was the large foam hand with the index finger raised indicating John was #1.

In the confusion and excitement, I forgot where we were and what we were doing and inadvertently placed a cigarette between my lips and struck one of those large wooden kitchen matches to light it. The timing couldn't have been worse on my part. As the young blonde designated victim reached around and undid her bra, she looked up to see Greg and I only a few feet away in our window grinning from ear to ear in the warm glow of the lit match like two jack-o-lanterns at Halloween. I knew exactly what she was seeing because Greg and I could see our own reflections in our own window. And it was a sight. We made quite an impression, beer in hand, sitting in the dark, both in our underwear, noses virtually pressed against the glass.

It actually took a few seconds for the young blonde to put together what she was seeing. Even though two thick panes of glass and about eight feet separated us, the subsequent scream made it seem like she was sitting next to Greg and me on our sofa. In a flash, the blond scooped up all of her clothing in one motion from the floor and was in a dead run in the direction of the door she had been escorted through just a few moments earlier. Mr. Hefner (John), bathrobe and all, quickly emerged from the bedroom and was in hot pursuit not knowing what had happen.

Having finally caught up to her as she reached his car, he was unsuccessful in persuading her to return, even to a different room of the house and had to take her home wearing his robe. The following day, Greg and I expected to hear about it from John but we never did. We did however get to admire John's new verticals curtains he had installed in his living room window.

There were many memorable parties and goings on at O.P.E.C.. But by far the biggest bash was Scotty's bachelor party. Scotty was one of the original Seven, so it had to be grandiose. We put the word out early on so the married guys and those who may as well have been married could start rehearsing their stories and out and out lies so they could attend. Our neighbor, John, was forewarned several days in advance of the event. He thanked us and sensed what was coming and booked his usual room at the Holiday Inn for a three-day stay this time.

Next was the entertainment committee. Big decision there, strippers! The girls at the local strip joint knew all the local cops and some of us more than others. The girls were delighted and all agreed to attend and some said they would even bring some new girls that were thinking about getting into the business. Where better to break in a new routine and a crisp dollar bill? Next was prepping the house for the girls and festivities. Tool box in hand, I made a trip next door, (the opposite side from John) to a home that was being demolished and removed every door in sight from its hinges and brought them back to O.P.E.C. With them, I was able to make a stage/runway that was in the shape of a "T" that filled our living room and extended out onto the porch and into the yard by the beach. There was also a sound system overhaul and a D.J. booth with colored lights, strobes and of course, a spot light. There were two or three kegs of beer and who knows what kind of hard liquor and mixing materials at the bar. We were now "locked and loaded"!

Scotty's bride-to-be was a sweetheart. She didn't give him the business about his party at all. She knew all of us and had been with him, and us, through the academy and had developed immunity towards the Seven by then. But there were other wives and girlfriends and they were a different story. I never really knew how women networked until then. As soon as one wife found out about the bachelor party and who was throwing it, the news spread like a fart in an elevator. The number estimated to attend went up and down as we got closer to the party depending on the number of domestic brawls. No one's arm was twisted to attend that I could recall. But it was unwritten that those who didn't make the party might as well show up at work the following day after wearing a paper sack over their heads wearing a dog leash. It was 'show up or be shamed!'

On the day of the event, several spent the entire day at O.P.E.C. just getting primed. The department had a terrible time finding people who would work because everyone took time off to attend. Around towards the end of the day, bodies started to filter in and seats around the runway were being claimed and the music and beer started to flow. In the next few hours, cars cluttered the driveway and spilled out onto the road in both directions. Police units that had the misfortune to have to work were also invited to drop by and high fives greeted new arrivals as they entered O.P.E.C.

Around dark, the girls started to arrive and were shown to their dressing room, (Greg's bedroom) while some mingled and served drinks. Most of the girls brought their own music and all were ready to get it on! It was nice to know that Greg and I didn't have to worry about any security deposit or damage to the house. It was going to be bulldozed anyway for a new condo. It was a good thing too. It was amazing how much damage a little alcohol and a few people can do to a wooden structure. We were all among friends and brothers and trusted that no matter how intoxicated we got, we knew that we would be looked after. We'd be talked about for a long time maybe but looked after nevertheless. The event soon took on the personality of a drunken Roman fiasco. Bodies littered the beach and yard and reports of a few shots fired later on in the evening filtered in to the department. Later we were told that someone had accidentally shot a hole through the floorboard of their car as they were leaving and one or two other partygoers had minor fender benders on their way home or getting out of our driveway but nothing serious. A couple of girls got left behind and once located the following morning had to be driven home by Greg and I. Greg had an especially memorable trip half way to his destination and had to return home. But as Forest Gump would say, "That's all I got to say about that". By all accounts, Scotty party was a success. But the true measure of the success of a bachelor party is the fallout that follows!

Within hours, the floodgates opened releasing a torrent of rumors and accusations lodged by wives and outraged girlfriends toward O.P.E.C. and Greg and I. The complaints ranged from drug usage to prostitution and bestiality. A close eye was kept on the activities of police and non-police present for obvious reasons and I didn't recall any animals present at the party and neither did Greg. In reality, a lot of people had a great time and a lot of harmless steam was blown off. And that just pissed some people off I guess? I lost track of the actual number of domestic separations and damaged relationships that resulted from Scotty's party, but it was a very respectable number.

O.P.E.C. continued for quite some time after Scotty's bachelor party. Spring breakers and women vacationers from all over were a common sight at the house on the beach. At one point, in order to save a little money otherwise spent on hotel accommodations, Greg and I would allow vacationing college girls to utilize our basement/garage as a place to stay during their break. For a while, we had girls sleeping on everything from the bench press to the washer and dryer. Life was good!

Down Time

It seems like the more job related stress there is, the more need there is for an outlet to get rid of that stress. That holds true for any occupation. Few will argue the buildup of stress is without a doubt, a killer in every sense. This holds true in law enforcement more so than most occupations. Stress wrecks ones physical health as well as mental health, and everything in between.

For some reason, I was fortunate in that most of the people I worked with had little problems locating that outlet valve that released that tension. Living and working in South Florida meant you had a lot of cool things to do in your down time. One fall day, Sergeant O'Reilly advised several of us that he had acquired a hand full of tickets on the fifty-yard line of a Dolphin football game in Miami. The tickets included a bus trip to and from the game and the bus would pick us up and drop us off just a few blocks from headquarters. What more could one ask for? It was a Sunday evening game; so around noon all but O'Reilly met at O.P.E.C. and started drinking heavily in preparation for kickoff scheduled at 7 p.m.

We were to be at the designated bus stop at around 5 p.m. and O'Reilly said something about bringing our own refreshments, but we weren't real clear what the definition of refreshments meant. So when 5 p.m. rolled around, there were half a dozen highly intoxicated off duty police officers with gallon jugs of Rum Runners and other concoctions in hand standing on the corner of Park Road and Lake Ave. We didn't have to wait long before a yellow school bus rounded the corner and came to a stop to let us on board. O'Reilly's smiling face met us at the bus door but the smile quickly changed to horror when he saw the condition of those about to get on board. O'Reilly had neglected to inform us that the bus excursion was provided and sponsored by his and his wife's church! You'd think that little detail would have been worth mentioning?

Too late now, we were on board and we were hammered. The trip to the stadium was tense. As intoxicated as we may have been, we still tried to appreciate the position our sergeant had placed himself in. The return trip was a different story however. The Dolphins had played the Jets and traditionally every New Yorker residing in South Florida attends these games. Half of those in attendance wind up in fistfights with Dolphin fans before they get out of Miami. Simply put, there was no love lost between the Dolphin fans and the Jet fans so there was a good chance you were going to either witness a good scrap or be a part of one. As it turns out, a couple from our group wound up being involved in one of those altercations at the game and was a little worse for wear when it came time to leave the game.

By anyone's standards, we were very drunk by early afternoon that day. So by the time we boarded the church bus for the return trip home from Miami, some had to be assisted to their seat where they slept quietly in their nasty soiled and beer soaked clothing. At some point during the ride home, a parishioner opened a brown grocery sack containing lunchmeat sandwiches and began to pass out snacks and cans of soda to other church members on the bus. As one male member of the church retrieved his sandwich from a fellow parishioner, he passed the seat of Officer Sample who was for the most part minding his own business and was polishing off what was left of a gallon jug of Rum Runner he had brought on board earlier. Officer Sample was ex-navy, (a submariner to be exact) and was never really *"right"* after spending nearly a year cooped up in a sub under the arctic ice pact.

As the male parishioner passed Officer Sample, he made the comment loud enough for everyone to hear, "God help us if this is an example of our local law enforcement!" Even intoxicated, Officer Sample realized that this wasn't a flattering comment and immediately took offence and stood up and yelled, "Let he who is without sin cast the first stone you Bible banging bastard!"

Up until then, I thought violence was something that was avoided by religious people. You know, the turn the other cheek thing? I guess it doesn't always apply and this was one of those occasions. The scrap was brief and broken up quickly but the rest of the ride home resembled an episode of Jerry Springer. O'Reilly had a lot of explaining to do with the wife when the congregation voted to kick them out of the church the following Sunday. I think when all was said and done; Mr. and Mrs. O'Reilly were mediated down to being put on probation of sorts at the church and Mr. O'Reilly was banded from any more Dolphin games that year. The Dolphins had a terrible season that year anyway!

Relieving stress came in many forms and increments large and small by every rank within the department. The use of horseplay for relieving stress wasn't reserved for just the patrol level officers. For example, there was some sort of sexual harassment complaint lodged against a captain in charge of the detective division by a female detective assigned to him. The allegation went as follows.

The captain of detective's office was located in a hallway directly across from a supply closet that contained forms for the detective's daily work. The captain's desk faced the door to his office and it looked directly at the supply closet door across the hall. This certain female detective assigned to the division was always locking horns with the captain over anything and everything. So to further aggravate the female detective and blow off some steam himself, the captain placed her paperwork on the bottom shelf making her have to bend over every time she retrieved the necessary forms. When she did and the captain saw her, the captain would grunt like some wild animal having sex, which would infuriate the female detective to no end. This evidentially made the captain feel much better. My, how things have changed!

Sometimes, stress relief can come in the form of surrogate gestures. What I mean is someone can do or say something toward the object of your frustrations and make you feel a lot better. For example; for a while the patrol division and the administration were at each other's throats constantly and it seemed like the patrol officers were always being dumped on and after awhile it really got old. The first Wednesday of every month at eight o'clock in the morning, the administration held their monthly staff meetings upstairs in the conference room around the chief's nice mahogany conference table. For the meetings, amenities like fresh coffee and several boxes of donuts were brought in fresh for their enjoyment.

During one of these staff meetings, as the donut level in the donut boxes went down, someone noticed a Polaroid photo at the bottom of the box. When the photo was removed and examined, it clearly showed the frontal view of a naked white male standing with his hands on his hips but you could only see from his neck to his knees in the photo. Normally this wouldn't have been a big issue but in this instance, the only thing the individual was wearing was three donuts! When the chief asked who brought the donuts to the meeting, everyone looked at each other and had thought the other had brought them. At first it was suggested by several angry staff members that every white patrol officer be stripped and subjected to a line-up in an attempt to identify the person in the Polaroid, but the chief's departmental legal liaison quickly blew that out of the water. It was clear that patrol division was behind the prank and had fired a shot over the bow of the administration letting them know we weren't happy with the status quo. From then on, no one under the rank of lieutenant was allowed to bring food or drink to staff meetings. To this day, I can't help but smile when I see a donut.

There are many kinds of stress in the workplace and the law enforcement profession offers a special variety of its own. The obvious kind of law enforcement stress is the life and death versions. Some stress inducing examples are *the man with a gun or shots fired* call or the foot or vehicle *pursuits*. These kinds of calls can make your palms sweat and heart race like a jet engine. At times, I've actually been able to hear my own heartbeat in my ears going to these calls. Every call can be a potential stress-producing death sentence. Then there are the more mundane types of stress like, late paperwork stress, media related encounters, supervision responsibilities, off duty conduct issues, courtroom testimony, civil and criminal liability issues etc.

Every waking minute, a law enforcement officer is under the gun and stressed out. Just knowing that anything you say do or imply may cause a negative and/or devastating effect on one or more people including yourself is enough to send most people over the edge. My advice to anyone who is considering law enforcement as a career would be to learn how to cope with stress first thing. If you don't, the future will certainly be a dismal one! Don't ignore stress! Don't bottle it up! Don't let those who work around you dump their stress on you either! And for God's sake, don't take it home! But the most important thing in dealing with stress is to have and nurture a good sense of humor.

Law enforcement is not without its risks. On another hot afternoon, a call went out over the radio that a drive-by shooting had just occurred. The dispatcher then gave out the description of the vehicle involved and its occupants. Within a few moments, I had located the vehicle that was parked and unattended at a local run down park in the heart of a bad neighborhood. The park had about seventy-five to a hundred people in it, half of which had active warrants. In any case, I radioed in that I had located the vehicle involved in the shooting and soon five or six other officers including a K-9 officer joined me.

Any accumulation of police will generally attract a crowd. And when a crowd gathers in these urban neighborhoods, a few within them will always try to incite the others into a mob frenzy and attempt to provoke the police into an altercation. This is a common ploy if for no other reason, just for the entertainment value. The previous occupants of the vehicle and the participants of the drive by shooting were among the crowd and had everything to gain by causing such a disruption and driving off the cops. In just a few moments, the crowd had gathered around the hand full of officers. They soon began their taunting and threats along with an occasional hurled rock and bottle. The instant the first officer took action and made an arrest, the riot was on!

First things first, a distress call was sent out over the radio that officers were in trouble and needed help. After that, we tried to keep from being separated from our guns, radio, and each other. Then we circled the wagons, went back to back and tried to hold out until the Calvary arrived. By the time the first back-up patrol units arrived, several officers including myself were in a fight for our lives type of bar room type brawl. Before the arriving officers could reach me, I had been hoisted over the head of a rioter by my neck and crotch and slammed down back first on the trunk of a parked car resulting in half my equipment on my duty belt flying off resulting in several broken ribs. However, on the "bounce", I managed to get my attacker around his neck and hold on long enough for him to be taken to the ground and eventually taken into custody by other officers. He turned out to be seventeen years old and one of the shooters and only got a slap on the wrist by the courts for the shooting and my injuries. I got a month off to heal up. As long as it is work related, most departments were pretty sympathetic and generous when it came to giving injured officers time off because of injuries. It always pissed me off when I'd see media footage of the big bad police beating some defenseless citizen for no apparent reason at one of these riots. They never showed footage of the bleeding and battered cop being dragged away to safety by his fellow officers after he got his head bashed in from a brick or bottle. It was and still is a tough job. And a day off here and there doesn't hurt anyone if it's needed.

Your Support

If one is leaning toward law enforcement as a career, do yourself a favor. Talk in depth with several others who are currently employed by the agency or branch of government you're interested in being employed by. Try and get a feel for how pleased they are with how their administration treats them. Go back several years and get a good history. Politics change every few years and so do the politicians and working conditions. I've been employed by four different agencies in my thirty years and each are as different as night and day in many ways.

The first agency was dominated and influenced by racial motivators common during that time period in our history. It was bearable only because crime was so out of control, we were too busy trying staying alive to notice most of the injustices and smaller things that get noticed by slower agencies. The upside of that agency was the pay and the benefits were good and we were located in one of the nicer areas of the country.

The second agency was a totally different animal altogether. It had a lower crime rate, but was dominated by the kind of politics that come with a middle class retirement/

Jewish type community. It was explained to me early on that the police and their dark uniforms reminded some of the older citizens of the days of WWII and the dreaded German Gestapo. Some citizens were openly hostile to anyone who wore a uniform of any kind. I tried to understand it and was as tactful and comforting as I could be, but the general population's attitude spilled over and was reflected in the attitude of the local government and city council. In short, the police got little support in any way shape or form. And if an opportunity arose to stick it to the local police department, it was usually utilized and implemented.

Within a two-year period, South Florida experienced several devastating hurricanes. These hurricanes decimated the infrastructure of the state as well as many municipalities. When it was determined that a hurricane was imminent, law enforcement was placed on alert. Our agency's hurricane protocol was that once alerted, all officers would come to headquarters (leaving their families and homes) and bring enough equipment and clothing for at least a three-day stay. We would then patrol two per vehicle and answer emergency calls only to prevent looting and perform any life saving duties as needed.

The mayor, city council and department heads would also respond. But here's where the difference between the police department and the others mentioned stood. The members of the police department had no emergency generators so we had no electricity and no air conditioning and had to sleep in the police department on the floor. The humidity was so bad, puddles formed on the dirty rain soaked carpet and it soon became moldy. The administration had their own new reinforced building with air conditioning and they slept on new cots complete with mattresses and had washers and dryers to keep the bedding nice and crisp.

We had to leave our families and homes to fend for themselves during the hurricane. The administration got to bring all their families INCLUDING THEIR PETS to their shelter.

The administration had food stacked to the ceiling including fresh vegetables, bakery products, steaks and even lobsters brought in for them. They had a full kitchen and two full time cooks. For the sixty officers, there were some boxed pasta, some crackers a coffee pot and some canned meat. It got to the point where officers were sent out to scavenge up what ever they could (during the storm) in order to feed the working officers. When one of the officers confiscated "one" of the three bar-b-q grills to cook some hot dogs on the administration had stashed for them, the mayor himself threatened to fire those responsible. After it was all over and we were able to go back to our homes and families, several of those who were privileged enough to stay with the department heads and council during the hurricane complained of picking up weight and being spoiled and depressed having to return home. The officers on the other hand were tattered and worn completely out. I don't think I've ever seen a more disgraceful display of selfishness and hypocrisy in my entire life from any group of people let alone a local government.

Engage but Detach

One of the biggest challenges in law enforcement is figuring out how to become involved enough to be effective yet detached enough to not be affected by negative outcomes.

As I've mentioned, my Achilles' Heel was the children. Maybe it was because I've always been a big kid myself or maybe it was because my youth was like so many that I dealt with on the streets. When the young and innocent fell victim to circumstance or were brutalized by those who were suppose to be their protectors, I couldn't help but feel as if I had let them down in some manner. The guilt would sometimes be overwhelming.

In the mid 90's, my main assignment was to direct/oversee a large juvenile athletic program for my agency. While doing so, I bonded with hundreds of youth from within the community. Some had little or no concerns that warranted intervention or guidance from me or any of my staff. But others came from broken homes riddled with drug and alcohol abuse. Others were physically abused or neglected to the point where they slept where they could and ate what they could find. These young adults cried out for attention and love and they took it from anyone who cared to extend a hand. From this group, I lost three my first year. It seemed like I was always standing next to a casket embracing young people and trying to comfort them as they filed by. And if I was asked once, I was asked a thousand times, "Why?"

Jose was an energetic twelve-year-old Latino lady's man. He had a smile that went from ear to ear and he could light up a room by just walking in and flashing those pearly whites. In the evenings, Jose would hang out at my boxing facility mainly to project the macho image that he thought the girls liked. He would dress out from time to time but he never really gave it his all. And after school, he would drop by and talk for a while and share his report cards with me and we would talk about the world and far away places. No one suspected what Jose was forced to go home to.

Jose lived with his mother and father in a small trailer along a dirt road not far from the gym. His mother and father were both illegal aliens but Jose was born in the United States. His father worked construction and his mother took in wash and cleaned homes for extra money. However, Jose's father was a drunk. He wasn't just a drunk; he was an angry drunk. On payday it was common for Jose's father to purchase a bottle of liquor and polish it off before going home. Once he arrived, Jose's mother would voice her displeasure and a violent domestic fight usually resulted. It was like this every Friday evening at Jose's home. But Jose never mentioned it to anyone. This had been going on for so long, I guess he thought it was like this for everyone and it was just natural. This Friday was to be different.

Jose's father arrived home at his usual time and in his usual belligerent and intoxicated state. And as usual the mother said just the right things to set him off again. This time, while Jose's father choked his mother with one hand, he reached in his pocket with his other and pulled out a small caliber handgun he had obtained that day and was waving it in Jose's mother's face threatening to kill her. Terrified that he was going to lose his mother, the twelve year old boy wedged his way between the two, pleading with his father not to harm the mother. As the drunken man pulled the boy from between the two adults, the gun discharged and Jose fell to the floor mortally wounded, blood pouring from a wound to his head. Jose's short life was over before he came to rest on the floor of the old and cluttered trailer.

Word reached me within minutes because it was commonly known that Jose frequented the boxing facility and most knew he had ties with program and its director Sergeant Smith. When I received the call and was informed by another officer of what had taken place, it was is if I were dreaming. I happened to be at home at the time and I suddenly found myself forgetting what I was doing and found myself in some sort of void where everything just didn't make sense. Then time seemed to stop and I felt myself feeling vulnerable and helpless. As a hardened officer, death becomes part of your everyday routine. To a veteran cop, death is nothing more than a state or category that means you'll need some specific official form or paperwork and have to set in motion some protocol. But now, it meant something else. I then realized that I had forgotten what death really was and that someone, a person, a human being, was gone.

After Jose's funeral, the staff of the facility met and we tried to find a way to shake off or minimize the loss of this beautiful child, especially under the tragic circumstances. Everyone including the staff was taking the loss very hard. The next morning when I opened the facility and made my traditional pot of coffee, I stepped out of the back door to drink it and felt the early morning warm Florida breeze on my face. There, I said a prayer asking for help. I asked that God send the staff and me someone or something to help us get through this loss so we could continue helping the kids the best we could. If they saw us suffering and unable to cope, it would surely trickle down to those who were younger and also suffering and unable to cope and would make things even worse. It felt strange that I was in a situation that I had no control over. I mean after all, the cops are called when all others lose control and my job was to restore order and take control. And until now, I thought I did my job rather well.

After the prayer and cup of coffee, I stepped back into the building and into the empty facility with its empty boxing ring, heavy bags and weights. Then I saw the main entrance door open and an Albert Einstein looking kind of gentleman step into the room. As our eyes met, I introduced myself and asked if I could be of assistance. The bearded gentleman said in a calming voice that he had heard of our youth program and had heard many good things about it. He also said he resided nearby and was an LCSW, (licensed clinical social worker) and would like to offer his services as counselor to the program. He then asked if I thought his services could be of any benefit to those who volunteered their time or the youth within the program. I smiled and told him I was expecting him but I didn't think he would arrive this soon. Puzzled, he looked at me as I poured him a cup of coffee and I explained.

A.J. was a senior in high school. He was another one of my boxers that kind of went through the program for the illusion or to give the impression he was a boxer. A.J. had problems fitting in and getting the needed attention that young people desperately require at school from their peers. He wasn't a "standout" at anything in particular. He came from the regular broken home and he made so-so grades. He had few true friends and no regular girlfriend. All he really had was a decent looking car with nice rims that made him envious by several peers. A.J. did find a way to make himself popular by his senior year however. He sold pot. A.J. was the "go to" guy for a nickel or dime bag of pot for those who smoked at school. It made him popular and it made him a few dollars and most of all he thought it made him cool. A.J. thought that buying an ounce or two of pot a week and breaking it down to smaller nickel and dime bags and selling them at a predominately white middle class high school couldn't get you in much trouble.

This went on for quite a while and midway in his last year, A.J. had fallen into that drug culture that doesn't really care what color you are or how little you're involved with drugs. In some circles, a white kid hanging out with black and Latino kids and riding around in a nice car getting high was all it took to appear cool. A.J.'s pot source dried up one week and two of his black "peeps" suggested that A.J. purchase his weekly supply of pot from their source that lived just a few blocks further into a bad section of town. The neighborhood was crime ridden and black but he would have two "brothers" along with him. So with nothing to be afraid of, A.J. agreed and the three were off to the "projects".

For some unknown reason, A.J.'s two "friends" wanted to utilize the back rout into the multi unit dwellings. At the end of a long deserted desolate stretch of road they arrived at their destination but knocks on the apartment door went unanswered so the trio returned to A.J.'s vehicle and they started back on the road they came.

Just a few hundred yards from the alleged drug house, one of the black males brandished a handgun and ordered A.J. to pull the car over to the side of the road. There, they ordered A.J. from the vehicle, took the few dollars A.J. had in his pocket, told him to get on his knees, and while A.J. pleaded for his young life, they shot him twice in the face. A.J.'s body was found the same day and his car was located that same evening behind the garage of one of the suspects in an alley. The rims and tires had been removed and the rest of the vehicle had been abandoned. A seventeen-year-old young man had forfeited his life for a set of chrome rims and a few dollars all because he wanted to look cool and be accepted.

A couple of days after the incident and after the medical examiner had completed his investigation; A.J.'s body was turned over to a local mortuary for burial. Once again, I found myself asking myself if there was anything I could have done to prevent this? I knew A.J. was involved in drugs but I failed to look close enough to realize the degree and act. I tried to convince myself that there was really no reason for me to feel that I should bare any guilt. I had nothing to do with his death. Yes, I had noticed on several occasions that A.J. had come to the facility high. And yes, I had heard that he sold pot at school but that was the school's responsibility. And then I stopped and thought, I saw the signs and I could have spoken up more than I did. I could have pitched the biggest damn fit or pleaded or begged or reasoned or just been there for him if nothing else. I knew I owed someone an apology.

Within an hour, I was at the mortuary and was talking to the director whom I knew. There, I asked to see A.J.'s body. I was told that no makeup or preparations had been done but I said it didn't matter. The director took me to a room I was familiar with and he left me alone with A.J.'s body.

I'd seen lots of deceased people and lots of them with gunshot wounds. Some looked horrible and some didn't. I swallowed hard and pulled the sheet back exposing the ash colored face of A.J. There wasn't much trauma. It appeared to look like a small caliber gun was the weapon of choice. I could only detect two small entry wounds. I didn't know exactly how I would react as I drove to the mortuary earlier but I was confident that there wouldn't be an emotional "break down" of sorts. After all, I was that harden cop and this was just another day at the shop.

As I looked at his face, I wondered what A.J. was thinking when he knew his life was about to end. Was he remorseful that he had gotten into that life style? Did he cry for his mother? Or did he do the "gangster" thing and take it like a man? About this time, things I wanted to say to A.J. started to pour into my head. Things that I wanted to tell A.J. about drugs, his family, his future and education. Then I thought why didn't this desire to intervene come earlier? Maybe, just maybe A.J. would still be here? I placed my hand on A.J.'s cold arm and apologized once more before I left the room. As I drove back to work, I promised myself that the mistake I made with A.J. would never repeat itself again, ever!

The last young man I lost was "Snickers". Yes, "Snickers". His real name was James. He too was a senior in high school. He was black and I believe from the Haiti. What a great kid. On the weekends, he would help his father at the local flea market selling clothes and gaudy gold plated jewelry that the kids liked. His grades were good and he was never in trouble at school or with the law. His mother spoiled him as any mother would who was blessed with a son like James.

James was a regular at the recreational facility but only in the halls. One day, a boxing coach who had seen James several times just hanging around asked if he would be interested in boxing. James was quick to point out that he was a lover and not a fighter. It was explained by the instructor to Snickers that boxing is not fighting. But James stood his ground and continued to spend his time idle hanging out in the halls. Several days passed and as the coach and I passed James in the hall again, the coach told me he saw something in the young black kid but just couldn't put his finger on it. The coach also told me about the lover verses the boxer conversation he had had with James. I asked the coach to let me give it a try.

As I approached James who was destroying a snickers candy bar at the time, he smiled and said, "Hello Sergeant Smith." I said, "James, I see you here in the halls every day it seems like. What gives"? James confidently replied, "It's a good way to meet girls." I said, "I understand the coach here asked if you'd be interested in the boxing program and you said no. Haven't you ever watched boxing on the television? Those guys have to beat the women off with a stick. Everyone knows the babes think boxers are the sexiest things on Earth," I explained.

That is pretty much all it took. James followed us into the gym and we couldn't get rid of him after that. To "chum" for the girls he wore boxing jewelry, boxing t-shirts and hats and eventually became a very accomplished amateur competitor. Because of his love for snickers candy bars, he was tagged with the ring name "Snickers" for the rest of his short life. It even caught on and became his name at school and at home.

Because Snicker's mother loved and spoiled him so much, his mother would occasionally allow him to drive the family's new Lincoln SUV to school. This made Snickers even more desirable to all the young girls on campus and Snickers eventually hooked up with a young attractive sophomore girl and both became an item. As the relationship grew, she would come to the gym from time to time and watch Snickers work out and would hover over him and treat any minor bump or scratch.

For some unknown reason, one day after school, Snicker's girlfriend wanted Snickers to let her drive his mother's SUV home from school, or at least close enough to where they could switch once they were close. I'm sure Snickers knew this was an unwise decision and I know he had to have resisted at first. But she was insistent and Snickers was a soft touch so she took the wheel prior to leaving the school parking lot. During the drive home, all appeared to be well until another motorist pulled in front of the young girl causing her to panic and swerve to her left across the median and into oncoming traffic. The driver of the oncoming semi tractor-trailer didn't have time to even hit his breaks. The SUV and large truck met head on and both Snickers and his girlfriend were killed instantly.

Weeks after the accident, Snicker's mother continued to grieve like no other I had ever seen before. And to this day, ten years later, when I see a Snickers candy bar, the edge of my mouth curls upward into a half grin and I think of the cheerful smile and warm heart of that sixteen-year-old kid we took out of the halls of the recreation center. And I remember how natural he took to an eighteen by eighteen foot boxing ring. The kid was genuinely all heart.

Your Number

Everyone's heard of the old adage, "When your number is up, it's up". This couldn't be truer than in law-enforcement. The Grim Reaper can rear his head on duty or off. It can come at the grocery store or at your mailbox getting your morning mail. On a warm summer morning several years' back, a woman came into the lobby of our district headquarters asking for an officer. I happen to be close by and was available so I swung by and offered my assistance. The woman explained that her husband had been taking prescribed medications and for some reason it had caused him to become very unpredictable and prone to severe mood swings. There was no mention of any violence or threats towards anyone or any reason to be overly cautious. The woman went on to explain that the family physician had signed papers to have the husband taken into custody and placed under observation until the problem was resolved but her husband was being uncooperative and refused to go. Therefore, she was requesting that law-enforcement take him into custody and deliver him to the nearest mental health facility under what's refereed to as a "Baker Act" in most states.

This wasn't uncommon and two officers usually handled calls of this nature without incident. According to the woman, her husband was at their home watching television and was refusing to be committed for observation. There was just one problem however. Their address was just outside our district's borders and needed to be handled by the district just to the north of ours. With commitment papers in hand, the woman calmly had a seat while I called for a deputy from the appropriate district to meet her in our lobby and handle her needs.

A short time later, a deputy arrived and I filled him in on what was going on. His name was Jimmy and I had met him on several occasions over the years. Jimmy was a young guy, about mid thirties with a big smile and even bigger mustache.

If you didn't know him, you'd swear he sang in an old fashion barbershop quartet because of the mustache. After hearing the woman's request and reviewing her paperwork, Jimmy called for a second deputy to meet him just a block away from the woman's residence so both could approach the man in his home. I also told Jimmy that I would go and be close by in case the man gave him any problems. You just never know. The back up deputy for Jimmy was a deputy I had trained about ten years prior. His name was Gregory and was as bright as they come. Gregory had come from a predominantly black high crime area and he knew the streets well and could be depended on without reservation. Of all that I had trained in the year's prior, Gregory was by far my favorite.

The address of this call was in a somewhat rural area where all the homes sat on a minimum of one and one quarter acre lot. It wasn't agriculture but it wasn't the suburbs either. It was where people that liked getting away from the city would settle down and enjoyed their yards and pets. As

Jimmy followed the woman complainant to her residence, I followed Jimmy and once we reached the boundaries of the two districts, I fell back and parked under a shade tree in case I could be of assistance. The house was less than a quarter of a mile away and I could be there is less than a minute if needed. As I sat under the tree, I proof read some reports and closely monitored the police radio for any sign of trouble.

As Jimmy and the woman approached her home, Gregory arrived and pulled his vehicle just behind Jimmy's. Jimmy filled Gregory in on the details and Gregory agreed to go to the rear of the home in case the man ran out the back door in an attempt to flee. After asking the woman complainant to remain with the patrol vehicles, Jimmy cautiously approached the front of the home. The home was a modest single story structure with natural wood siding and had an SUV parked in the gravel driveway directly in front of the house about thirty feet from the front door. Jimmy took up a tactical position directly behind the SUV being careful not to expose himself unnecessarily. From there, he could see that the home's screen door was closed but little more beyond that due to the lack of light inside the home. With his sidearm drawn and to his side, Jimmy raised his voice loud enough (but calmly and politely) and asked for anyone inside to please step outside so he could speak to them. Jimmy's request went unanswered. Jimmy repeated the request again and once again, silence.

By now, Gregory had opened the back door and was slowly making his way (gun drawn) through the kitchen and toward the living room that was located in the front of the home and where the disturbed man was thought to be. Gregory had heard Jimmy's requests but knew little more and moved forward slowly. Not knowing why his requests were not being answered, Jimmy moved to the driver's side of the rear of the SUV and took a peek around the corner of the vehicle to get a better look to see if anyone was in the doorway or to detect any possible movement. That was Jimmy's fatal mistake.

The disturbed man had loaded his 30-30-caliber lever action rifle and was standing just inside the screen door waiting for this opportunity. When Jimmy peeked around the corner of the vehicle, the man took careful aim and fired. The 30-caliber bullet tore through the screen door and struck Jimmy just above his left eye. The result was devastating. Jimmy was dead before his body hit the ground.

Hearing the shot but not knowing exactly what had taken place, Gregory took his last few steps and rounded the corner and now had a view of the living room and the disturbed man standing in front of the screen door that he had just fired through. With his back toward Gregory and still clutching the gun, the man suddenly sensed Gregory's presence and turned. After several stern commands by Gregory to drop the smoking rifle, the man finally complied and lowered his gun to the floor. Gregory now instructed the man to step from the living room out onto his front steps with his hands raised and behind his head. There, Gregory expected to find Jimmy waiting to help take the man into custody. Instead, as Gregory and his prisoner stepped from the house and out into the yard, Gregory was horrified to see his friend and fellow deputy face up and obviously dead lying in the gravel driveway still clutching his sidearm. That's when all hell broke loose!

We are taught early on that our most important piece of equipment is not our gun but our radio. Without it, we are on our own and at the mercy of anyone or anything. Not only is it vital for our wellbeing, we cannot aid others if we can't hear them. It is, in effect our lifeline, period! Over time, we learn to listen to the radio much like we listen to our children. It's not so much what is said but how it's said and any background noise also contributes to the message. And as a supervisor, I particularly paid attention to any stress I may detect. As I sat in my vehicle reviewing reports, the radio suddenly barked out every officer's nightmare. In Gregory's frantic and distressed voice, I heard, "Alpha 7, 10-24, 10-24, officer down". Alpha 7 was Gregory's call sign and the ten code, "10-24" meant that an officer was down and/or was in deep shit! I could also hear in between words the rustling of bodies and heavy breathing indicting that a struggle was taking place.

Every law enforcement officer's ears that that transmission fell upon instinctively and immediately dropped what ever they were doing, found a vehicle, commandeered a vehicle or hitched a ride with someone in a vehicle and was in route to Alpha 7's location "balls to the wall". And God help anyone or anything that got between them and the officer calling for help. In my case, I knew Gregory well and knew the sound of his voice and detected serious trouble even before he had ended his transmission. I threw my paperwork to one side and dropped my vehicle into drive, activated the overhead lights and siren and simply pointed the patrol vehicle in the direction of Gregory and floored it. The less than thirty second ride seemed like an eternity. The radio was now was choked with other supervisors barking out instructions to air and ground units desperately trying to get someone, anyone to Alpha 7's location.

As I rounded the corner and onto the dirt road where the deputies were, I could see both Jimmy's and Gregory's green &white patrol vehicles parked along side of the road with the woman complainant kneeling and covering her face near them. Then I saw Gregory on the ground struggling with the disturbed man trying to handcuff him in the yard between the two homes. I steered my vehicle off the road and onto the grassy yard toward Gregory. With the wheels locked from mashing on the breaks, I threw the vehicle into park sliding to within a few feet of the two men. With the vehicle still sliding, I swung the driver's door open, exited and was in the fray assisting Gregory. Within a few seconds, the disturbed man was finally secured in handcuffs and I was able to pause and see various pieces of Gregory's equipment (including his radio) scattered about the yard indicating that the struggle, however brief it had been was violent. Out of breath and with a torrent of tears streaming down his face, Gregory raised his head and pointed toward the SUV and muttered, "He's dead, Jimmy's dead". I stood and ran towards the SUV and found Jimmy, laying on his back, eyes still open and clutching his revolver. It was obvious that nothing could be done so I returned to Gregory who was kneeling next to the man who had just taken Jimmy's life for no reason. The look from Gregory was that of a child to his mother that had just endured some horrific trauma that he couldn't bear or understand. And as the tears continued to stream down Gregory's face, all I could do was kneel next to him and take him into my arms, rock him like a child and repeat over and over that everything would be ok.

Within seconds, the dirt road we were on became an unbreathable cloud of dust with dozens of red and blue lights and sirens from a steady flow of marked and unmarked vehicles from various agencies answering the call for help. And from above came the familiar chopping sound of the sheriff's helicopter along with a few from the media.

At that point in my career, again I considered myself somewhat hardened and resistant to stress brought on by job adversity and crisis. But to this day I don't remember being separated from Gregory by anyone. I only remember being walked back to my patrol vehicle by a plain-clothes detective cradling my arm in his. There I was seated in the driver's seat with my feet outside the vehicle on the grass as the detective rubbed my shoulders while he guarded over me keeping the media at bay. As I sat there with my head in my hands, I could look to my right and still see the body of Jimmy that was now partially covered by a yellow plastic emergency blanket that someone had taken from their trunk's equipment box. To my left, I could see Gregory in the rear of an ambulance being tended to by paramedics and comforted by the department's Chaplin.

For the next few moments, I wondered many things. I wondered who's body would have been under that yellow blanket if the woman and crazy man had lived just a few homes further down the street and into my district? Then I wondered how Jimmy's now widowed wife would receive the news? And how would she break the news to their two young children? Then I wondered why anyone would want to do this for a living day after day? I was kind of ashamed when the answer came to me. It was because most cops were simply addicted to it. No less than a junkie to his dope or a drunk to their booze. Then I thought, God help us!

To Protect and Serve

"To protect and serve" isn't just some slogan or catch phrase that looks good painted on the side of patrol vehicles. If you are in law enforcement, you are the closet representative of the government to the people. Unlike congress, the mayor, or even a councilperson, the public can reach you 24/7. They can flag you down any time they need to. And at times, knock on your door if the need is urgent. If one ever does choose this profession, I hope and pray that they utilize and take advantage of the position to its fullest.

There are six kinds of cops. The first I call the "***Cookie Cutter Cops***" because they are all alike. To be hired (as I explained earlier), he/she will tell an "oral review board" of how they want to serve the community and do something meaningful with their lives. They will tell of how they want to help humanity and do their part and contribute to society. Then when hired, they'll answer the radio and handle calls in a manner just enough to clear the call and move on to the next call. And when they patrol, they look straight ahead and see little going on around them. I've been behind these people driving in traffic when a call goes out near to them. To dodge the call, they'll not get on the radio to advise they are near the location of the call and will abruptly take a side street out of the area and try not to be seen making others come from a further distance to handle the incident and what should have been their work.

The second is the "***Big Fish in a Little Pond***" cop. This guy/gal is simply too bright and has too much experience to trouble themselves with the every day mundane calls for service. They are to be utilized for the big and important stuff. Let everyone else take the routine calls. They can be found with their feet up on someone else's desk and can usually be heard before they are seen. They also usually have a jacket full of complaints from the community. They love to give advice but are nowhere to be found when that advice turns out to be the wrong advice. Simply put, when it's time to move the piano, they're the first ones to grab the bench!

The third is the "***Organizational Terrorist***". No matter what you do, they are obligated to critique it. Oh they'll tell you to your face how great a job you did, but behind your back and to others, they just can't figure out how you manage to keep your job being such a bumbling idiot. Every profession has them but they really stand out in law enforcement.

The fourth kind is the "**Moo Cow Cop**". This guy/gal will milk a call or a detail until hell freezes over. Their meal breaks are always extended burdening others with their workload and they will not bat an eye when doing so. Their cars always need gas or repair of some sorts taking them away from their duties and when they show up on your calls and they'll stand around doing nothing so they can later say they were tied up assisting you.

The fifth kind of kind of idiot you'll be dealing with is the "***Butt Plug Cop***". If any kind of supervisor stops suddenly, this guy/gal will instantly become a "butt plug" because they always have their heads up someone's ass! They just can't seem to do enough for the boss, but seldom get their own work completed. These people will know the boss's office better than the boss. And if they think they can advance themselves in some manner by ratting out someone or undermining others efforts, they'll do it! You will find them in conversations they have no business in and in unexplainable places. These people usually find themselves mysteriously being appointed by supervision to serve on boards and panels with everyone wondering what the hell are they doing there? Anyone with more intelligence or more qualified are considered a threat and are quickly demeaned and maligned because the "butt plug" sees them as a threat and will quickly move to eliminate them from the competition.

And finally, there's the *"Real Cop"*. This is the person that you hope and pray will show up to your family's home if they are in need and you can't be there. This cop listens, cares, is helpful, and treats your family like they are his/hers. This cop will gladly give what he or she has and will not make mention of it to anyone wanting recognition or favor for it. This cop doesn't consider what he or she does as work but rather a means to contribute. They take pride in what they do and comfort in knowing that their reward is a good night sleep.

A **Real Cop** lets their superiors know that their instructions need only be given once and need not be checked and rechecked on the quality or timeliness of the task given. And when in doubt, the Real Cop will seek advice from those who issued the task and not from those who would just render a guess or feeling. There will seldom be complaints or negative feedback from the general public on this cop yet occasional praise will trickle in from the same public. If a concern or complaint is brought to the table by a real cop, this cop will generally bring one or more possible solutions along with them. In short, these officers are usually the standard for others around them. To become one of these officers is easy. Simply care for others and enjoy what you're doing.

The View Looking Back

It's common while in law enforcement (as well as the fire fighting profession), to have young people approach you and ask questions about the profession and ask for your recommendation as to which of the two career paths would you recommend for them? Having a lot of fire fighting friends, I made it a point to poke fun at their profession at every opportunity. If a firefighter friend was close by and I was ever asked the difference between the two professions, I'd tell the inquiring person that a firefighter only had two decisions to make a day: The first being, what are we going to Bar-B-Q today and second being, what movie are we going to rent? That usually got the ball rolling and the doughnut jokes started.

Both professions are noble ones and have their own unique risks and rewards. But unlike firefighting, law enforcement issues are most always human behavior (make that "bad" behavior) related in origin. In police work, nearly every serious call resulted in an arrest and someone unhappy with the cops for some reason. But in contrast, nearly all encounters with fire personnel ended with the public thanking the firefighters for their efforts and showing up.

And as the fire personnel drove off in the sunset; the public would shower them in fresh baked pastries while blowing them kisses. That's why you can always find fresh baked pies and cakes over at the fire department's kitchen. It's a wonder any of them can squeeze into a fire truck! In the kitchen of the local police department however, you'll find a single pot of day old coffee strong enough to patch a pothole and an open can of Vienna Wieners.

I always dreaded being publicly recognized along with a firefighter. Sometimes a firefighter friend and I would do something like yank an unconscious kid from a local swimming pool/canal or burning building and we'd be requested to appear at a local council meeting to receive a life saving letter or plaque. When we're recognized and the firefighter's occupation is announced, there's would be applause and cheer. And when my occupation was announced, there was usually a smattering of applause and there was always some idiot that just got arrested for domestic violence or issued a traffic ticket booing in the back row. We all want to be recognized for our efforts and when we're not, it leaves a vacancy in our psyche that needs to be filled. Too often, officers tend to isolate themselves from coworkers and family and each day on the job is nothing more than another nail in their coffin. These people tend to look at the world around them as if every encounter was a "call" to be handled. And before long, everyone outside of work and family are divided into two categories, "suspects" and "victims." Once this occurs and this attitude becomes the norm, it is all downhill from there.

Not too long ago, all one had to be to become a police officer was to be big and not too bright. You were literally handed a gun and a night stick and if you were lucky, a patrol car and told with the point of the sergeant's finger that, "This is your area. Now go and keep order!" Today, college degrees and spotless backgrounds and references are what most credible agencies are looking for. Constitutional law, state laws, civil law, physiology, sociology, political science, and a litany of high liability issues are covered in academies nationwide. The days of the non-specialized, uneducated law enforcement officer are fading fast. If one thinks that law enforcement is anything like what's depicted on the television as, think again.

The profession is an ever changing and improving science. It is a study of what works and what does not in order to achieve a specific goal or outcome. Mix in some politics, political correctness, and some serious ass kissing from time to time and you have law-enforcement. It is a profession that in order to be successful, all you have to do is survive to fight another day. I was asked not too long ago, in my three decades of law enforcement: "What did I learn in three decdes and what was I proud of the most"?

Well, I can tell you this. By far, most of my career was that of a road sergeant. And I'm proud to say that in all that time, not one single officer under my supervision, (**not one**) failed to make it home to his or her family safe and sound after their tour of duty. Yes, some of us had to be stitched up or put back together with pins and plaster but at least we were home with our families at day's end. Some supervisors were seldom seen and spent their time in the office or just made themselves available only if you called for them. The street was where I felt I was needed and I tried to be as close as I could to my people and I went on as many calls as I could for backup if nothing else. And what I learned is nothing more than common sense.

I learned that teaching family values and work is necessary but not nearly enough. In order to reduce crime, the government ***must end welfare paychecks for immoralities***! Crime is the direct outgrowth of a growing moral breakdown of society. The consequences of this phenomenon are undeniably catastrophic. Children from broken homes are far more likely to do poorly in school, use drugs, require psychiatric attention, and commit crimes than those in equally low-income homes where a ***father is present***. And the crimes that they commit grow increasingly vicious as their moral understanding of the value of human life disintegrates. If you do finally decide that law enforcement is the path for you, let me give you a little advice.

First and foremost, if you do not have a sense of humor, develop one quickly and nurture it daily! This will absolutely and undoubtedly be your lifeline to sanity and any hope of a successful life by any standard. Without actively seeking a little levity while working in the bowels of depravity, you will soon become what you are exposed to. By having a sense of humor and practicing it regularly, you separate yourself from the horrors of humanity long enough to enjoy that retirement you've worked so hard for.

Second, be very careful who you surround yourself with on and off the job. While on the job, steer clear of those who always seem to be giving advice or are criticizing other officer's performances. These people climb the structural ladder by dragging others down as oppose to advancing themselves by their own merits and achievements. You'll usually find these people with their feet propped up on someone else's desk and you'll hear them long before you see them as you walk the halls of work. They're quick with the advice but nowhere to be found when that advice turns out to be sour. And when you finish your work, they always seem to be around to tell you how "they would have done it better". These people are called "organizational terrorist" and act as what a "boat anchor" would keeping the organization from moving forward.

Third, when off the clock, try and find yourself **non-law enforcement** people to hang with that appreciate what you do and understand the position you're in. It will be difficult but they're out there and well worth the effort. They will keep you stabilized and help you keep things in their proper perspective. You do not want to detach yourself from the world and all it has to offer. For as much misery and negativity the world has to offer, there is an equal amount of good and beauty provided for our well being by someone who really cares about you.

Forth, the sun does not rise and set on your job. And that goes for any job. It is just that, a job! You are not on any "crusade" of sorts and the world will not come to an end if you choose to change your vocation or decide that the cost is just too high. And by too high, I mean that if your marriage/family or your physical or mental health is at risk, move on! Many officers do not finish their careers due to health problems brought on by job stress or end their careers only to quickly fall victim to those health issues induced by years of stress. These issues include stroke, heart attack, diabetes, overweight, mental illness, alcoholism, drug addiction, and a lengthy list of other serious issues that can make their later years less enjoyable than what they deserve to be. In other words, take care of number one! I was lucky; the only residual physical effect I took with me from three decades of being on the job was a slightly curved spine and a ruptured L-4 and L-5 vertebra from wearing a gun belt that supported twenty four pounds of "essential" crap on it. I also have in my filing cabinet several x-rays and M.R.I.'s that will support the war stories that I'll share with my buddies around the campfires and on bar stools.

Fifth, this is not a one size fits all world. You'll be told in the beginning that you will have to metaphorically wear a variety of hats in order to function as law-enforcement. If you are lucky enough to work in a place where everyone is nice and respectful, disregard the following. But if you want to survive, chances are from time to time you will need to break out the "alter you."

This "alter you" is much like the one I worked with we called "Brain Damage". This is the officer that everyone fears simply because he's/she's appears to be nuts. Nearly every agency has at least one and they are the "go to guy" when the chips are down. Crowds part like the Red Sea when they walk, rooms get suddenly quiet when they enter and people crane their necks just for a chance to be witness to this person's next act of lunacy. And everyone's heard of at least one horror story (unsubstantiated of course) of how this cop has bitten an ear off or gouged an eye from someone's socket just for the fun of it. Respect is an unknown commodity on the streets. But fear is the universal lubricant that will let you move unimpeded when every two-bit wannabe gangster and loud mouth punk challenges others.

Lastly (and most importantly), be happy with what you're doing. Take satisfaction in knowing that what you are doing is "good"! What you do touches many lives and will be felt for years to come. Not many are given the opportunity to leave their footsteps in the sand. The years that have gone past seem like yesterday and when thoughts come to mind of those years, a smile always comes to my face. Even in my retirement, I've found it difficult to leave the profession entirely. I'm now a reserve deputy and a school resource officer (S.R.O.) at a local rural K to 12th grade school with just a few hundred students.

For me, life has gone from light speed to just a crawl. Now when a patrol vehicle speeds past with lights and siren wailing, for a moment I think in my mind that I too should be in that speeding vehicle barking out instructions over the radio to other responding units. But I've convinced myself that it's not my job any longer. I tell myself that I've done my share and it is time for me relax. It is hard, but I'm trying.

One would be hard pressed to find any other occupation that has the camaraderie, the hair-raising terror, the absolute hilarity and the profound reverence that is the soul of law enforcement. And if you are as fortunate as I was to have so many colorful characters and outright wonderful human beings as I had to call friends and coworkers, you my friend will truly be a blessed person!

God Bless and Take Care,
Sergeant Larry Smith (Ret.)

Sgt. Larry Smith is one of three children raised by a single parent in Indiana. After finishing high school, Larry enlisted in the Marines and later attended Ball State University. Because of nepotism and the "good old boy" system in his hometown of Muncie, Indiana in the late seventies, achieving his goal of becoming a law enforcement office was next to impossible. Not taking no for an answer, Larry got his chance working the dangerous streets of South Florida for the next twenty-eight years. After retiring in 2008, he moved back to the Mid-West and settled in Southern Illinois where he is currently a deputy assigned to a local rural school as their School Resource Officer (S.R.O.). He is also a member of a Narcotic's Task Force combating the methamphetamine, crack cocaine and illegal firearms epidemic.

LaVergne, TN USA
07 May 2010
181818LV00001B/7/P